The BRAINY BOOK of Addition and Subtraction

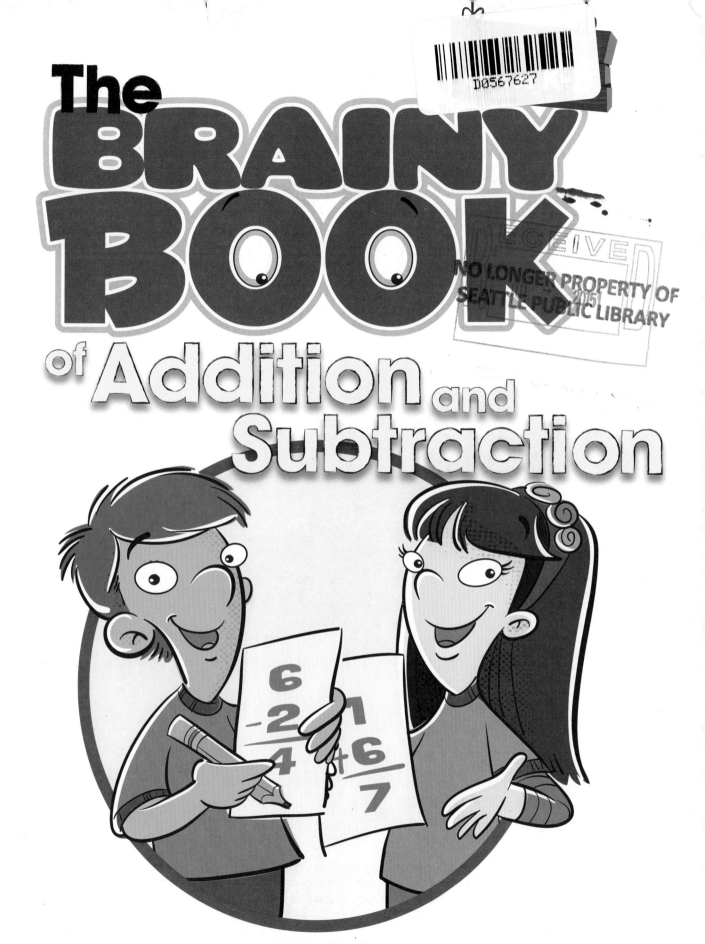

D0567627

RECEIVED
2015

NO LONGER PROPERTY OF
SEATTLE PUBLIC LIBRARY

Thinking Kids™
An imprint of Carson-Dellosa Publishing LLC
P.O. Box 35665
Greensboro, NC 27425 USA

Thinking Kids™
An imprint of Carson-Dellosa Publishing LLC
P.O. Box 35665
Greensboro, NC 27425 USA

© 2015 Carson-Dellosa Publishing LLC. Except as permitted under the United States Copyright Act, no part of this publication may be reproduced, stored, or distributed in any form or by any means (mechanically, electronically, recording, etc.) without the prior written consent of Carson-Dellosa Publishing LLC. Thinking Kids™ is an imprint of Carson-Dellosa Publishing LLC.

Printed in the USA • All rights reserved.
01-113157811

ISBN 978-1-4838-1326-4

Table of Contents

Table of Contents

Addition 1, 2

Count the dogs and cats. Then, write how many.

Buzzing Bees

Add to find the sum. Write each answer on a beehive.

$1 + 2 =$ 3

$2 + 3 =$

$3 + 2 =$

$3 + 1 =$

$1 + 1 =$

$2 + 2 =$

$2 + 1 =$

$1 + 3 =$

0 to 3

Add using the fireflies.

1 + 1 = __2__

$$\begin{array}{r} 1 \\ + 1 \\ \hline 2 \end{array}$$

2 + 1 = _____

1 + 2 = _____

2 + 0 = _____

$$\begin{array}{r} 0 \\ + 2 \\ \hline \end{array}$$

3 + 0 = _____

$$\begin{array}{r} 0 \\ + 3 \\ \hline \end{array}$$

0 + 0 = _____

$$\begin{array}{r} 0 \\ + 0 \\ \hline \end{array}$$

1 + 0 = _____

$$\begin{array}{r} 0 \\ + 1 \\ \hline \end{array}$$

Hearts and Stars

Count the shapes. Write the numbers below them to tell how many in all.

_____   _____   _____

- - - - - - -   +   - - - - - - -   =   - - - - - - -

_____   _____   _____

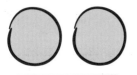   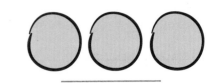

_____   _____   _____

- - - - - - -   +   - - - - - - -   =   - - - - - - -

_____   _____   _____

_____   _____   _____

- - - - - - -   +   - - - - - - -   =   - - - - - - -

_____   _____   _____

_____   _____   _____

- - - - - - -   +   - - - - - - -   =   - - - - - - -

_____   _____   _____

Addition 3, 4, 5, 6

Practice writing the numbers, and then add.

3 ------------------------

4 ------------------------

5 ------------------------

6 ------------------------

$$\begin{array}{r} 2 \\ +4 \\ \hline \end{array}$$

$$\begin{array}{r} 1 \\ +4 \\ \hline \end{array}$$

$$\begin{array}{r} 3 \\ +2 \\ \hline \end{array}$$

$$\begin{array}{r} 1 \\ +2 \\ \hline \end{array}$$

Addition Antics

Look at the pictures. Complete the addition sentences.

1 + 3 = _____

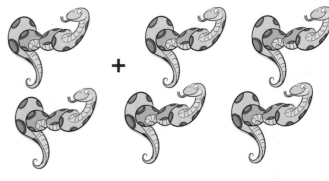

2 + 4 = _____

3 + 5 = _____

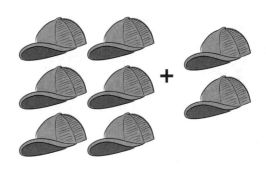

6 + 2 = _____

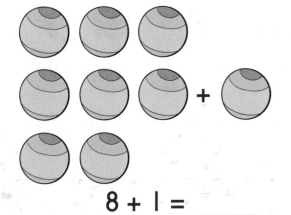

8 + 1 = _____

0 + 7 = _____

Button Up!

Add using the buttons.

4 + 1 = _____

2 + 3 = _____

$\begin{array}{r} 1 \\ + 4 \\ \hline \end{array}$

$\begin{array}{r} 3 \\ + 2 \\ \hline \end{array}$

$\begin{array}{r} 2 \\ + 2 \\ \hline \end{array}$

4 + 0 = _____

2 + 2 = _____

$\begin{array}{r} 0 \\ + 4 \\ \hline \end{array}$

5 + 0 = _____

1 + 3 = _____

$\begin{array}{r} 1 \\ + 4 \\ \hline \end{array}$

$\begin{array}{r} 3 \\ + 1 \\ \hline \end{array}$

How Much Candy?

Add using the pieces of candy.

   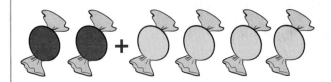

1 + 5 = _____   2 + 4 = _____

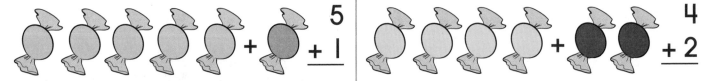

6 + 0 = _____

```
  0
+ 6
```

```
  3
+ 3
```

3 + 3 = _____

Lumberjack Facts

Add to find the sum. Use the code to color the picture.

Code:

1 — red	3 — black	5 — brown
2 — yellow	4 — blue	6 — green

Pet Picture Problems

Circle the picture that matches the addition sentence.

$1 + 2 = 3$

$3 + 2 = 5$

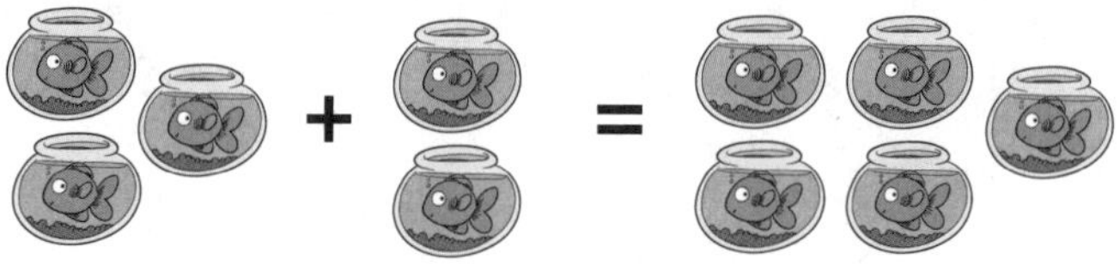

$2 + 4 = 6$

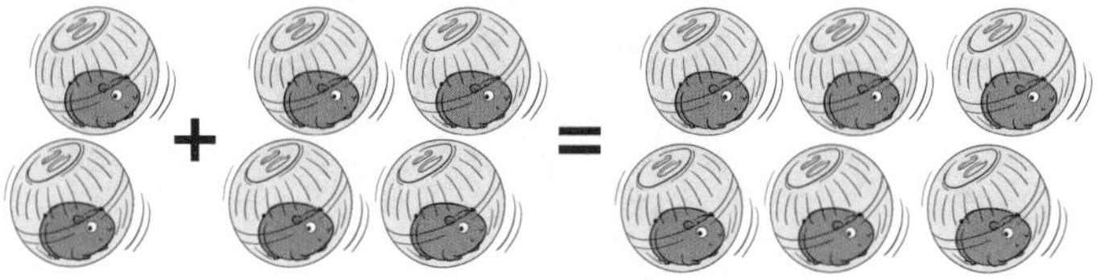

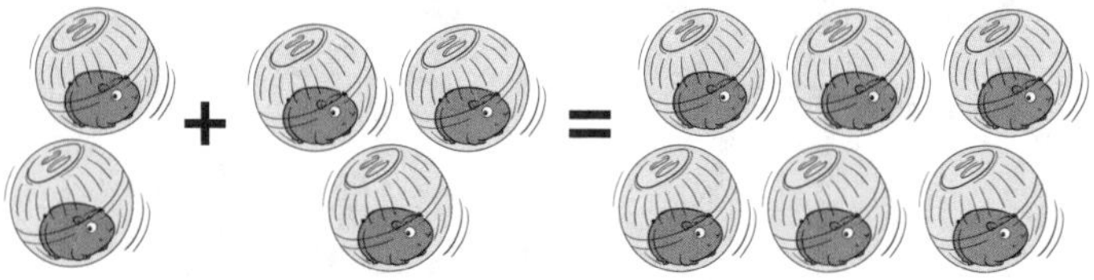

$3 + 3 = 6$

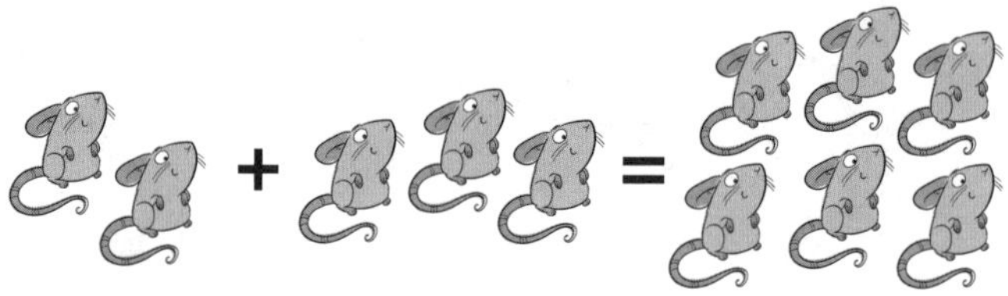

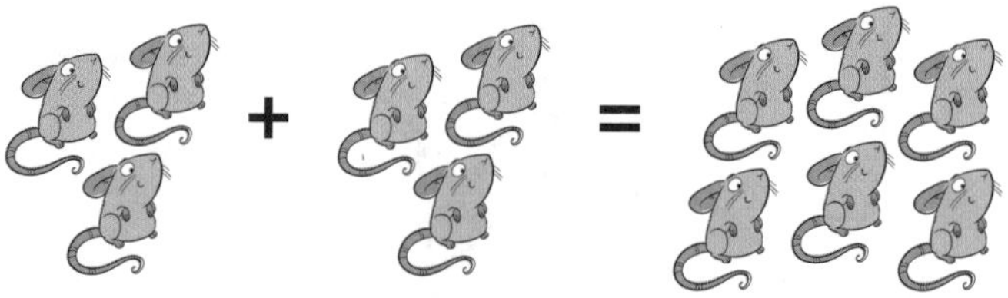

$3 + 4 = 7$

$1 + 6 = 7$

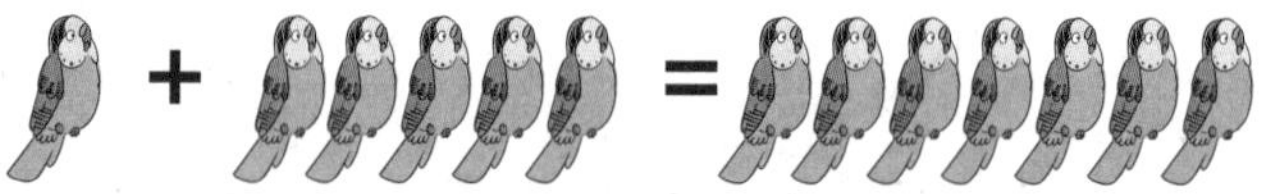

Addition 7, 8, 9

Practice writing the numbers and then add.

7 ------------------------------

8 ------------------------------

9 ------------------------------

$$\begin{array}{r} 8 \\ +1 \\ \hline \end{array}$$ $$\begin{array}{r} 3 \\ +5 \\ \hline \end{array}$$

$$\begin{array}{r} 2 \\ +7 \\ \hline \end{array}$$ $$\begin{array}{r} 6 \\ +1 \\ \hline \end{array}$$

Domino Decisions

Add using the dominoes.

$3 + 4 =$ _____

$\begin{array}{r} 4 \\ + 3 \\ \hline \end{array}$

$6 + 1 =$ _____

$\begin{array}{r} 1 \\ + 6 \\ \hline \end{array}$

$7 + 0 =$ _____

$\begin{array}{r} 0 \\ + 7 \\ \hline \end{array}$

$2 + 5 =$ _____

$\begin{array}{r} 5 \\ + 2 \\ \hline \end{array}$

Sum Flower

Add to find each sum.

If the sum is **6**,
color the area **blue**.

If the sum is **7**,
color the area **yellow**.

Domino Drill

Add using the dominoes.

5 + 3 = _____

$$\begin{array}{r} 3 \\ + 5 \\ \hline \end{array}$$

7 + 1 = _____

$$\begin{array}{r} 1 \\ + 7 \\ \hline \end{array}$$

2 + 6 = _____

$$\begin{array}{r} 6 \\ + 2 \\ \hline \end{array}$$

$$\begin{array}{r} 4 \\ + 4 \\ \hline \end{array}$$

4 + 4 = _____

Fresh Fruit Facts

Draw pictures to show what happens in each story. Solve the problem.

The monkey holds 2 s.

He has 8 s in the jeep.

How many s in all? _____

There are 4 s on the tree.

There are 3 s on the ground.

How many s in all? _____

The monkey picked 2 s.

There are 6 more s left on the vine.

How many s in all? _____

Bear Necessities

How many more are needed? Draw the missing pictures. Complete the addition sentences.

 +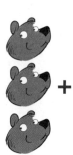

1 + _____ = 3

+ =

3 + _____ = 5

 + =

5 + _____ = 8

 + =

3 + _____ = 6

 + =

2 + _____ = 7

 +

4 + _____ = 5

Domino Domination

Add using the dominoes.

2 + 7 = _____

5 + 4 = _____

    7
 + 2

    4
 + 5

1 + 8 = _____

3 + 6 = _____

    8
 + 1

    6
 + 3

    0
 + 9

    9
 + 0

0 + 9 = _____

9 + 0 = _____

Robot Invasion

Complete the addition sentences.

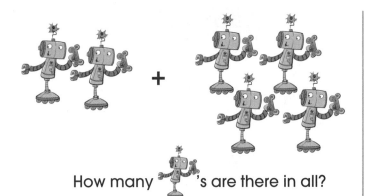

How many 's are there in all?

2 + 4 = _____

How many 's are there in all?

3 + 5 = _____

How many 's are there in all?

4 + 3 = _____

How many 's are there in all?

4 + 1 = _____

How many 's are there in all?

2 + 5 = _____

How many 's are there in all?

4 + 4 = _____

The Missing Chickens

Draw the missing chickens. Complete the addition sentences.

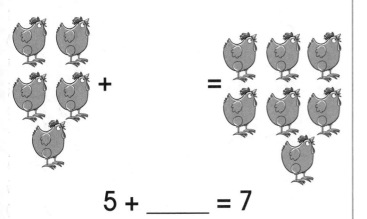

_____ + 2 = 3

_____ + 3 = 6

5 + _____ = 7

_____ + 3 = 5

_____ + 4 = 8

7 + _____ = 8

Air Bear

Help Buddy off the ground. Add to find the sum.
Then, color the clouds with sums of 9 to find the right path.

5 + 5 = _____

7 + 4 = _____

3 + 7 = _____

6 + 3 = _____

8 + 1 = _____

6 + 4 = _____

2 + 7 = _____

2 + 5 = _____

5 + 4 = _____

10 + 1 = _____

6 + 5 = _____

3 + 4 = _____

9 + 0 = _____

2 + 5 = _____

0 + 9 = _____

5 + 5 = _____

4 + 5 = _____

2 + 6 = _____

8 + 2 = _____

3 + 6 = _____

The Aliens Have Landed!

Complete the addition sentences.

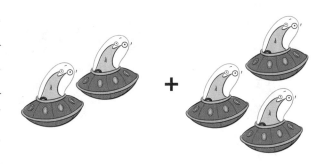

2 + 3 = _____

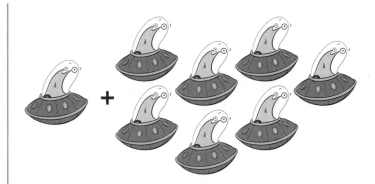

1 + 7 = _____

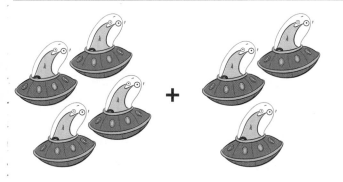

4 + 3 = _____

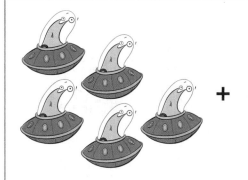

5 + 0 = _____

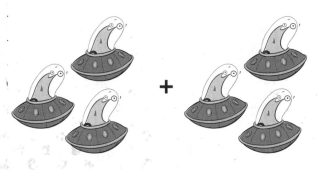

3 + 3 = _____

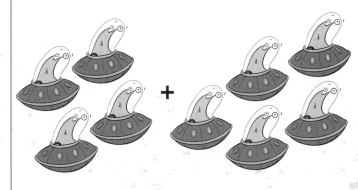

4 + 5 = _____

Rabbit Rascals

Complete the addition sentences.

How many 's are there in all?

1 + 1 = _____

How many 's are there in all?

3 + 6 = _____

How many 's are there in all?

6 + 1 = _____

How many 's are there in all?

3 + 4 = _____

How many 's are there in all?

4 + 5 = _____

How many 's are there in all?

2 + 3 = _____

Shape Sums

Add using the shapes.

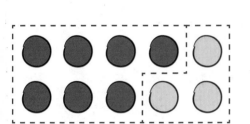

$$\begin{array}{r} 7 \\ + 3 \\ \hline 10 \end{array}$$

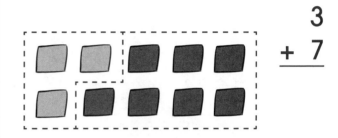

$$\begin{array}{r} 3 \\ + 7 \\ \hline \end{array}$$

7 + 3 = _____

3 + 7 = _____

1 + 9 = _____

2 + 8 = _____

$$\begin{array}{r} 9 \\ + 1 \\ \hline \end{array}$$

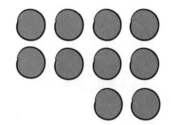

$$\begin{array}{r} 8 \\ + 2 \\ \hline \end{array}$$

6 + 4 = _____

10 + 0 = _____

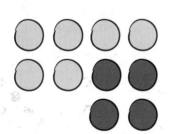

$$\begin{array}{r} 4 \\ + 6 \\ \hline \end{array}$$

$$\begin{array}{r} 0 \\ + 10 \\ \hline \end{array}$$

Alien Addition

Add to find the sum. Write each answer on a spaceship.

4 + 5 =

1 + 9 =

7 + 1 =

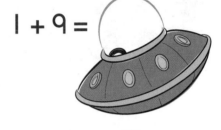

7 + 3 =

5 + 2 =

6 + 1 =

8 + 2 =

3 + 5 =

6 + 3 =

6 + 2 =

In the Doghouse

Complete the addition sentences.

2 + 6 =

7 + 3 =

6 + 1 =

4 + 5 =

6 + 2 =

7 + 2 =

Toucan? You Can!

Add to find the sums. Use the code to color the picture.

Code:

1 — white	2 — yellow	3 — orange	4 — purple	5 — red
6 — pink	7 — gray	8 — brown	9 — green	10 — blue

Brainy Book of Addition and Subtraction

Ready to Roll!

Roll a die. Write the number from the die in the top box. Add to find the sum.
Roll again to make each sentence different.

Counting Up

Count up to get the sum. Write the missing number in each blank.

3 + _____ = 6

4 + _____ = 5

7 + _____ = 9

2 + _____ = 4

3 + _____ = 8

5 + _____ = 5

8 + _____ = 10

7 + _____ = 8

6 + _____ = 9

8 + _____ = 9

4 + _____ = 6

6 + _____ = 6

5 + _____ = 7

4 + _____ = 7

9 + _____ = 10

5 + _____ = 8

7 + _____ = 10

6 + _____ = 8

Domino Dots

Count the dots on each side of the dominoes below. Write the addition sentence and the sum for each domino.

_____

_____

_____

_____

_____

_____

Name _____

Picnic Pests

The Barton family is having a picnic. But the ants have carried away their food.

Use an addition equation to find out how many ants took food. The first one is done for you.

How many ants carried away fruit?

$$\underline{\ 1\ } + \underline{\ 2\ } = \underline{\ 3\ }$$

How many ants carried away vegetables?

$$\underline{\quad} + \underline{\quad} = \underline{\quad}$$

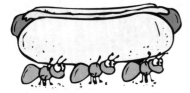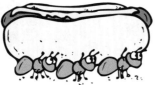

How many ants carried away hot dogs?

$$\underline{\quad} + \underline{\quad} = \underline{\quad}$$

How many ants carried away bread?

$$\underline{\quad} + \underline{\quad} = \underline{\quad}$$

34

Brainy Book of Addition and Subtraction

The Numbers Game

Roll the dice or cubes to find two addends. Write them on the first two lines.
Then, add to find the sum.

1. _____ **+** _____ **=** _____

2. _____ **+** _____ **=** _____

3. _____ **+** _____ **=** _____

4. _____ **+** _____ **=** _____

5. _____ **+** _____ **=** _____

6. _____ **+** _____ **=** _____

7. _____ **+** _____ **=** _____

8. _____ **+** _____ **=** _____

9. _____ **+** _____ **=** _____

10. _____ **+** _____ **=** _____

Solving Stories

Write a number sentence to solve each problem.

1. Brad ate 5 slices of pizza. Rashad ate 3. How many slices of pizza did both boys eat?

_____

2. Torika scored 4 points for the team. Danielle scored 4 points. How many points did

Torika and Danielle score? _____

3. Mischa bought 6 dresses. Desiree bought 3. How many dresses did they buy in all?

_____

4. 3 bears are having a picnic. 2 more bears join the fun. How many bears are having a

picnic now? _____

Sum Fun

Add to find the sum.

3 + 1	9 + 1	6 + 3	4 + 2	4 + 6	1 + 8	2 + 7
7 + 3	6 + 2	5 + 5	2 + 4	3 + 5	4 + 3	3 + 6
4 + 5	1 + 4	2 + 8	4 + 1	2 + 2	3 + 4	6 + 1
7 + 1	6 + 4	5 + 2	3 + 7	1 + 2	2 + 6	5 + 1
5 + 3	7 + 2	3 + 4	1 + 3	3 + 7	4 + 3	5 + 4

Fill the Grid!

Write the sums where the columns and rows meet. The first one shows you what to do.

+	1	2	3	4	5	6	7	8	9
1	2								
2									
3									
4									
5									
6									
7									
8									
9									

How Many in All?

Count the number in each group and write the number on the line.
Then, add the groups together and write the sum.

 _____ brushes

 _____ cookies

 _____ brushes

 _____ cookies

How many in all? _____

How many in all? _____

 _____ lollipops

 _____ puppets

_____ lollipops

 _____ puppets

How many in all? _____

How many in all? _____

 _____ balls

 _____ flowers

 _____ balls

 _____ flowers

How many in all? _____

How many in all? _____

Seeing Double

Roll a die and draw the dots in the box. Then, use the number to write a doubles fact number sentence. The first one has been done for you.

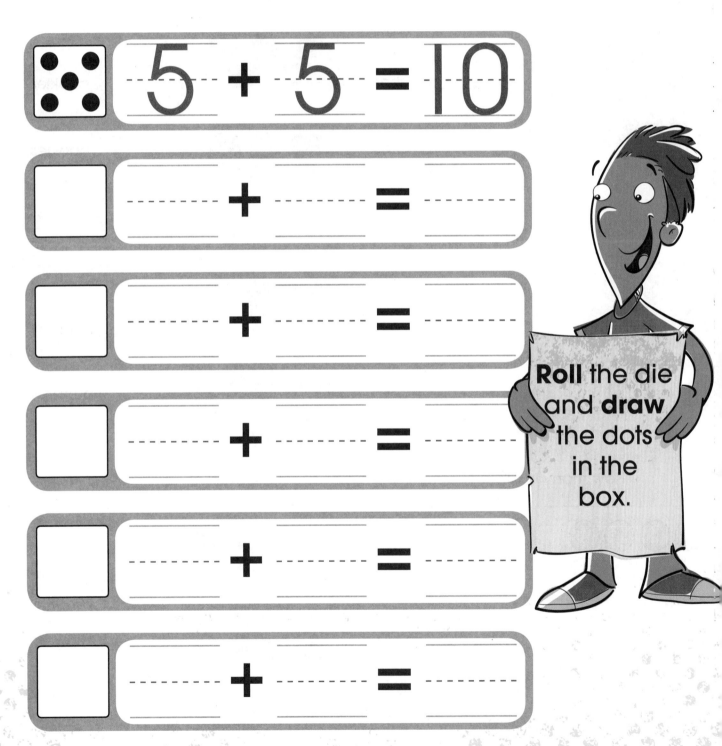

$$5 + 5 = 10$$

Roll the die and **draw** the dots in the box.

At the Zoo

Add to find the sum.

3 + 9 = _____   6 + 7 = _____   6 + 5 = _____

5 + 7 = _____   4 + 9 = _____   9 + 6 = _____

7 + 7 = _____   9 + 6 = _____   6 + 8 = _____

It's All the Same

Count the objects and fill in the blanks. Then, switch the addends and write another addition sentence.

If __**3**__ + __**8**__ = __**11**__ , so does __**8**__ + __**3**__ .

If _____ + _____ = _____ , so does _____ + _____ .

If _____ + _____ = _____ , so does _____ + _____ .

If _____ + _____ = _____ , so does _____ + _____ .

If _____ + _____ = _____ , so does _____ + _____ .

Add the Apples

Match the addition sentences with their sums.

8 + 2   15
9 + 6   4
2 + 2   10

1 + 2   11
6 + 7   3
5 + 6   13

3 + 2   10
6 + 8   14
5 + 5   5

6 + 2   8
1 + 1   6
1 + 5   2

7 + 2   15
6 + 9   9
12 + 1   13

6 + 6   12
6 + 3   9
3 + 4   7

10 + 1   14
9 + 5   8
7 + 1   11

Target Practice

Add the numbers from the inside out. The first one has been done for you.

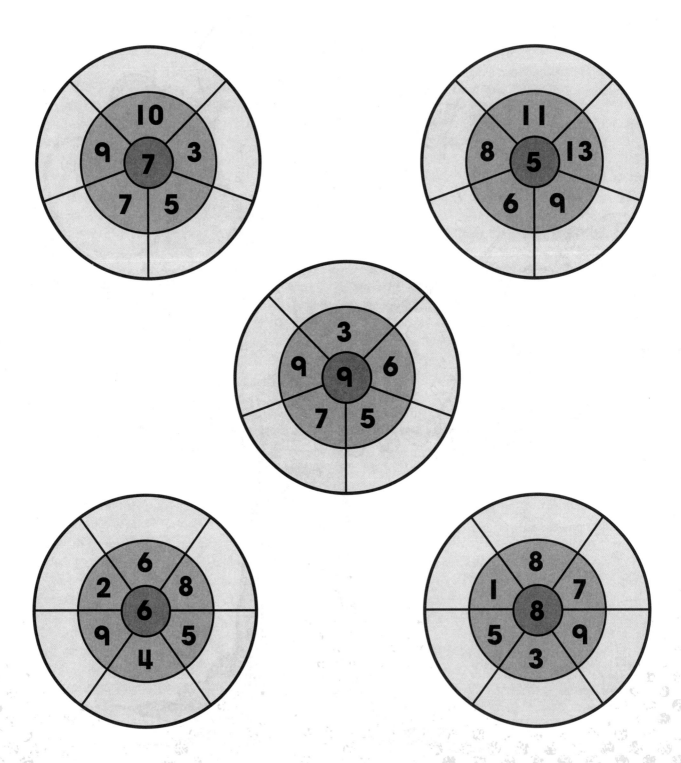

Catch Some Waves

Write each problem on the wave with the correct answer.

8 + 5	8 + 6	7 + 5	8 + 4	4 + 9
6 + 6	9 + 7	9 + 5	6 + 7	5 + 9
7 + 8	7 + 9	8 + 9	8 + 8	
6 + 9	7 + 6	5 + 8	3 + 9	
9 + 3	5 + 7	8 + 7	7 + 7	
6 + 8	9 + 8	9 + 6	9 + 4	

15 _____
_____

16 _____
_____

12 _____
_____

14 _____
_____

17 _____
_____

13 _____
_____

Brainy Book of Addition and Subtraction

45

Name _____

Bowls of Cherries

Three children picked cherries. Add the three amounts of cherries that each child picked.

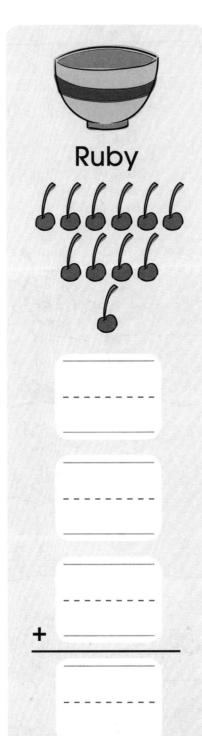

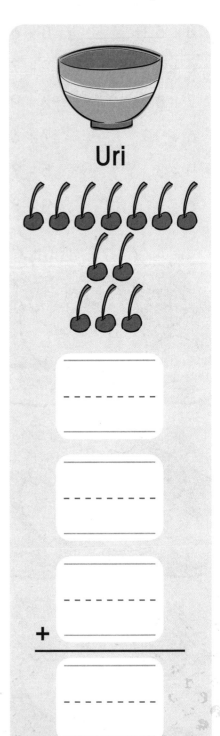

Brainy Book of Addition and Subtraction

Picking Cherries

Three children picked cherries. Add the three amounts of cherries that each child picked.

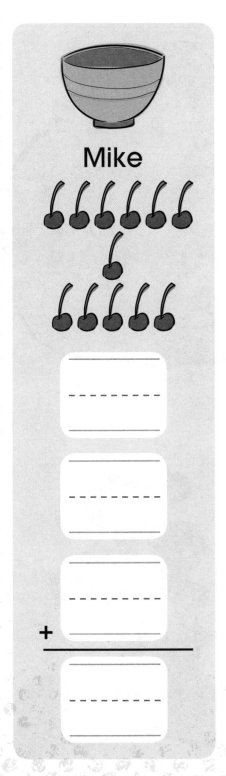

Math-Minded Mermaids

Look at the starfish. Then, look at the numbers. Circle each pair of numbers that can be added together to equal that number.

Number Detective

Find the missing numbers in the problems below.

$3 + \bigcirc = 14$

$12 + \square = 18$

$4 + \triangle = 17$

$9 + \bigcirc = 15$

$11 + \bigcirc = 16$

$8 + \square = 13$

$7 + \square = 13$

$9 + \triangle = 17$

$\bigcirc + 10 = 14$

$6 + \triangle = 16$

$\bigcirc + 3 = 12$

$\square + 2 = 14$

$\square + 3 = 12$

$\square + 7 = 10$

$\triangle + 9 = 18$

$\triangle + 8 = 15$

Bubble, Bubble

Add the numbers in the bubbles. Then, color the bubbles with a different color for each sum.

Adding Strategies

When adding three numbers, add the first two numbers first. Then, add the third number to the sum of the first two numbers. To decide which two numbers to add first, try one of these strategies.

Look for doubles.

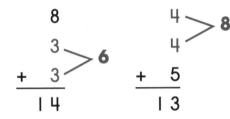

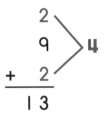

$$\begin{array}{r} 8 \\ 3 \\ + \ 3 \\ \hline 1\,4 \end{array} \quad 6$$

$$\begin{array}{r} 4 \\ 4 \\ + \ 5 \\ \hline 1\,3 \end{array} \quad 8$$

$$\begin{array}{r} 2 \\ 9 \\ + \ 2 \\ \hline 1\,3 \end{array} \quad 4$$

Look for a ten.

$$\begin{array}{r} 7 \\ 3 \\ + \ 4 \\ \hline 1\,4 \end{array} \quad 10$$

$$\begin{array}{r} 8 \\ 4 \\ + \ 6 \\ \hline 1\,8 \end{array} \quad 10$$

$$\begin{array}{r} 1 \\ 5 \\ + \ 9 \\ \hline 1\,5 \end{array} \quad 10$$

Add to find the sum of these numbers. Look for a 10 or doubles.

$$\begin{array}{r} 5 \\ 5 \\ + \ 4 \\ \hline \end{array} \qquad \begin{array}{r} 2 \\ 6 \\ + \ 8 \\ \hline \end{array} \qquad \begin{array}{r} 7 \\ 1 \\ + \ 7 \\ \hline \end{array} \qquad \begin{array}{r} 3 \\ 7 \\ + \ 4 \\ \hline \end{array} \qquad \begin{array}{r} 6 \\ 2 \\ + \ 6 \\ \hline \end{array}$$

$$\begin{array}{r} 7 \\ 6 \\ + \ 6 \\ \hline \end{array} \qquad \begin{array}{r} 7 \\ 8 \\ + \ 3 \\ \hline \end{array} \qquad \begin{array}{r} 6 \\ 7 \\ + \ 4 \\ \hline \end{array} \qquad \begin{array}{r} 5 \\ 5 \\ + \ 3 \\ \hline \end{array}$$

Add to find the sum. Show the detective the correct path. Color the path with sums of 13.

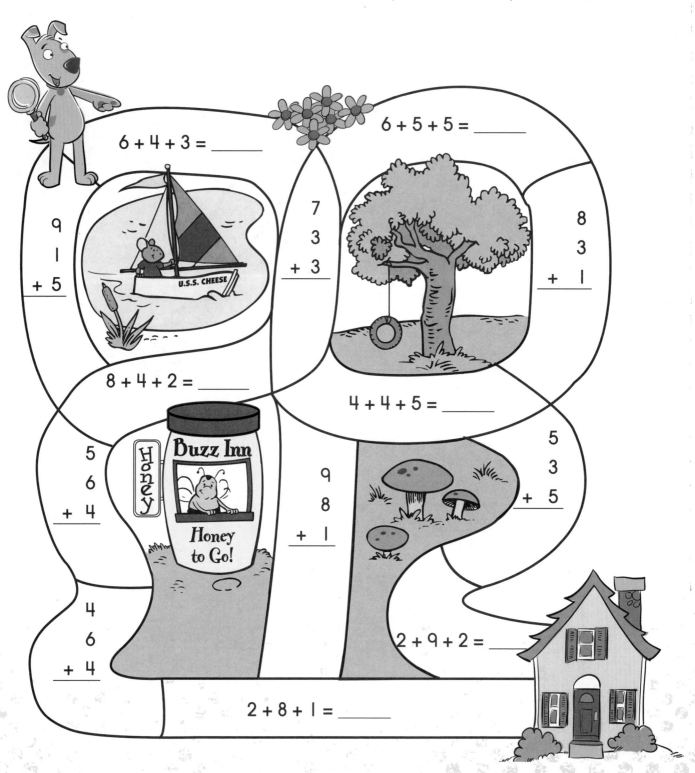

6 + 4 + 3 = _____

6 + 5 + 5 = _____

$$\begin{array}{r} 9 \\ 1 \\ +\ 5 \\ \hline \end{array}$$

$$\begin{array}{r} 7 \\ 3 \\ +\ 3 \\ \hline \end{array}$$

$$\begin{array}{r} 8 \\ 3 \\ +\ 1 \\ \hline \end{array}$$

8 + 4 + 2 = _____

4 + 4 + 5 = _____

$$\begin{array}{r} 5 \\ 6 \\ +\ 4 \\ \hline \end{array}$$

$$\begin{array}{r} 9 \\ 8 \\ +\ 1 \\ \hline \end{array}$$

$$\begin{array}{r} 5 \\ 3 \\ +\ 5 \\ \hline \end{array}$$

$$\begin{array}{r} 4 \\ 6 \\ +\ 4 \\ \hline \end{array}$$

2 + 9 + 2 = _____

2 + 8 + 1 = _____

Sweet Scoops

Add to find the sum. If the sum is 11 or more, color the cone brown. If the sum is less than 11, color the cone yellow.

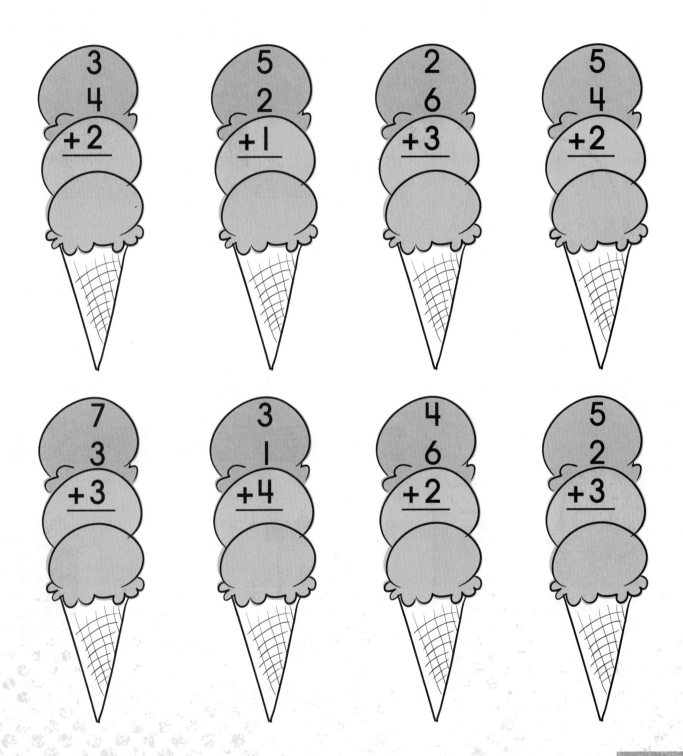

Zero the Hero

Write each missing number to complete the addition facts with zero.

$$15 + 0 = \underline{\quad}$$

$$15 + \underline{\quad} = 15$$

$$\underline{\quad} + 18 = 18$$

Plenty to Wear!

The key words "in all" tell you to add. Circle the key words "in all" and solve the problems.

1. Javier has 4 white shirts and 2 yellow shirts. How many shirts does Javier have in all?

   4 ◯ 2 = _____

2. Allison has 4 pink blouses and 6 red ones. How many blouses does Allison have in all?

   4 ◯ 6 = _____

3. Chang has 3 pairs of summer pants and 8 pairs of winter pants. How many pairs of pants does Chang have in all?

   3 ◯ 8 = _____

4. Jamaica has 2 black skirts and 7 blue skirts. In all, how many skirts does Jamaica have?

   2 ◯ 7 = _____

5. Jeff has 5 knit hats and 5 cloth hats. How many hats does Jeff have in all?

   5 ◯ 5 = _____

Adventure Island

Count on to solve each problem. The common sum is the spot where the pirate buried his treasure. Mark the spot on the number line with an X.

0 1 2 3 4 5 6 7 8 9 10 11 12 13 14 15 16 17 18 19 20

| 10 | 14 | 16 | 11 | 9 | 15 |
| + 8 | + 4 | + 2 | + 7 | + 9 | + 3 |

_____ _____ _____ _____ _____ _____

"X" Marks the Spot

Count on to solve each problem. The common sum is the spot where the pirate buried his treasure. Mark the spot on the number line with an X.

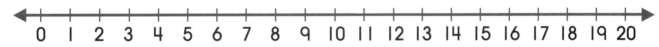

0 1 2 3 4 5 6 7 8 9 10 11 12 13 14 15 16 17 18 19 20

10	12	14	11	8	13
+ 6	+ 4	+ 2	+ 5	+ 8	+ 3

Ancient Adding

Roll a pair of dice. Write the number from each die on the lines below. Add to find the sum. Roll again to make each sentence different.

_____ + _____ = _____   _____ + _____ = _____

_____ + _____ = _____   _____ + _____ = _____

_____ + _____ = _____   _____ + _____ = _____

_____ + _____ = _____   _____ + _____ = _____

_____ + _____ = _____   _____ + _____ = _____

_____ + _____ = _____   _____ + _____ = _____

Camping Solutions

Add the numbers in each sleeping bag. Write the sums. Color in the four largest answers.

5 + 6 =

9 + 8 =

5 + 1 =

9 + 7 =

8 + 6 =

7 + 7 =

9 + 9 =

2 + 9 =

10 + 10 =

9 + 5 =

6 + 9 =

7 + 6 =

Zero the Hero Returns!

Write each missing number to complete the addition facts with zero.

$$11 + 0 = \text{\_\_\_\_\_}$$

$$\text{\_\_\_\_\_} + 0 = 16$$

$$0 + 20 = \text{\_\_\_\_\_}$$

You "Can" Do It!

Add to find each sum. Connect the dots in order. Use the sums and letters from the box to answer the riddle.

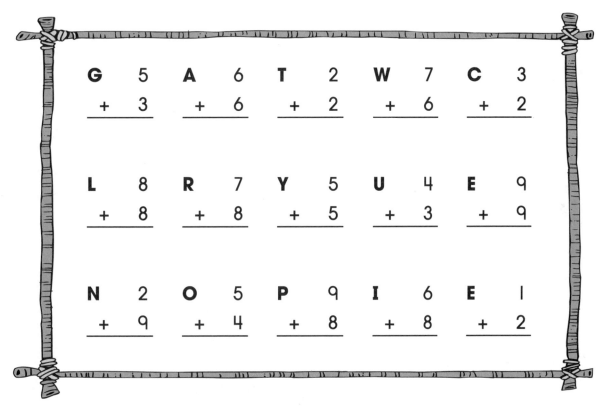

G	5	**A**	6	**T**	2	**W**	7	**C**	3
+	3	+	6	+	2	+	6	+	2
L	8	**R**	7	**Y**	5	**U**	4	**E**	9
+	8	+	8	+	5	+	3	+	9
N	2	**O**	5	**P**	9	**I**	6	**E**	1
+	9	+	4	+	8	+	8	+	2

Riddle: What do you get when you cross an eel and a goat?

___ ___ ___ ___ ___ ___ ___
10 9   7   13 14 16 16

___ ___ ___ ___ ___
8   18 4   12 11

___ ___ ___ ___ ___ ___ ___ ___
3   16 18 5   4   15 14 5

___ ___ ___
5   12 11

___ ___ ___ ___ ___ ___
9   17 18 11 18 15

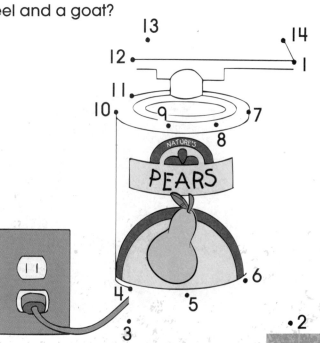

Racing Riddle

Solve each row from left to right. Write the letters on the lines below to answer the riddle.

E	3	H	2	S	4	Y	7	A	4	O	7
	4		9		4		9		5		7
+	7	+	1	+	7	+	3	+	8	+	2

B	9	P	8	T	9	I	5	V	6	R	9
	8		4		9		2		2		6
+	5	+	6	+	6	+	1	+	3	+	6

Riddle: What do a race car and a zebra have in common?

___ ___ ___ ___   ___ ___ ___ ___
22 16 24 12   12 17 11 14

___ ___ ___ ___ ___ ___ ___
15 24 21 8 18 14 15

Add and Laugh

Add to find the sums. Write the letters on the lines.

M $7 + 3 + 1 =$	M $7 + 0 + 2 =$	A $6 + 4 + 5 =$
C $5 + 6 + 3 =$	Y $2 + 2 + 6 =$	M $5 + 3 + 5 =$
M $8 + 2 + 7 =$	R $5 + 4 + 3 =$	Y $4 + 2 + 1 =$
U $8 + 3 + 5 =$	M $6 + 2 + 0 =$	U $8 + 1 + 9 =$

Riddle: What do you call a mummy who eats crackers in bed?

$\overline{}$ 15 $\overline{}$ 14 $\overline{}$ 12 $\overline{}$ 16 $\overline{}$ 9 $\overline{}$ 17 $\overline{}$ 7 $\overline{}$ 11 $\overline{}$ 18 $\overline{}$ 13 $\overline{}$ 8 $\overline{}$ 10

Race to the Top!

Roll a pair of dice. Color in the box that shows the sum. Which number got to the "top" first?

2	3	4	5	6	7	8	9	10	11	12

Problems in the Park

Write a number sentence to solve each problem.

1. At the park, there are 3 baseball games and 6 basketball games being played. How many games are being played in all?

_____

2. In the park, 9 mothers are pushing their babies in strollers, and 8 are carrying their babies in baskets. How many mothers in all have their babies with them in the park?

_____

3. On one team, there are 5 boys and 3 girls. How many team members are there in all?

_____

4. There are 8 men and 4 boys pitching horseshoes. In all, how many people are pitching horseshoes?

_____

5. While playing basketball, 4 of the players were wearing gym shoes and 6 were not. How many basketball players were there in all?

_____

Neighborhood Numbers

Write a number sentence to solve each problem.

1. On the block where Cindy lives, there are 7 brick houses and 5 stone houses. How many houses are there in all?

_____

2. One block from Cindy's house, there are 6 white houses and 4 gray houses. How many houses are there in all?

_____

4. Near Cindy's house, there are 3 grocery stores and 5 discount stores. How many stores are there in all?

_____

3. Children live in 8 of the two-story houses and 2 of the one-story houses. How many houses in all have children living in them?

_____

5. In Cindy's neighborhood, 4 students are in high school and 9 are in elementary school. In all, how many children are in school?

_____

Shining Stars

Add to find the sum.

3 + 3	7 + 4	9 + 6	5 + 6	9 + 3	4 + 6	4 + 8
5 + 5	5 + 8	1 + 7	9 + 3	6 + 8	8 + 9	5 + 6
5 + 9	7 + 3	9 + 4	3 + 6	2 + 8	7 + 6	4 + 5
8 + 6	3 + 5	5 + 7	9 + 9	8 + 6	8 + 5	6 + 7
3 + 8	8 + 7	3 + 9	9 + 8	7 + 4	2 + 4	4 + 3

Mystery Sums

Add to find the sums.

```
    2        6        4        5        5        7        3
+   9    +   6    +   9    +   4    +   9    +   7    +   5
_____
```

```
    9        5        9        6        8        9        9
+   9    +   8    +   8    +   5    +   5    +   6    +   4
_____
```

```
    4        8        9        4        5        4        9
+   4    +   6    +   7    +   6    +   3    +   5    +   9
_____
```

```
    7        6        7        3        8        4        6
+   3    +   6    +   8    +   8    +   3    +   3    +   7
_____
```

```
    3        7        3        8        5        6        2
+   2    +   5    +   4    +   8    +   2    +   3    +   6
_____
```

Time for Tens!

Add the tens.

$$2 \text{ tens}$$
$$+ \ 4 \text{ tens}$$
$$\mathbf{6} \text{ tens}$$

$$6 \text{ tens}$$
$$+ \ 2 \text{ tens}$$
$$\mathbf{8} \text{ tens}$$

20 + 40	60 + 20	20 + 20	10 + 50
40 + 20	30 + 40	50 + 30	30 + 20
60 + 10	20 + 50	70 + 10	10 + 10

10 + 20	40 + 40	80 + 10	60 + 30	20 + 60

Crack the Case!

Solve each problem.

Example:

There are 20 men in the plane.
Then, 30 women get in the plane.
How many men and women are in the plane?

$$\begin{array}{r} 2\,0 \\ +\ 3\,0 \\ \hline 5\,0 \end{array}$$

Jill buys 10 apples.
Carol buys 20 apples.
How many apples in all?

There are 30 ears of corn in one pile.
There are 50 ears of corn in another pile.
How many ears of corn in all?

Henry cut 40 pieces of wood.
Art cut 20 pieces of wood.
How many pieces of wood were cut?

Tens and Ones

Look at the example. Follow the steps to add.

Example:

```
   4 2
 + 2 4
 _____
```

Step 1:
Add the ones.

tens	ones
4	2
+2	4
	6

Step 2:
Add the tens.

tens	ones
4	2
+2	4
6	6

```
   3 3        1 5        3 8        1 1        3 7        7 2
 + 4 1      + 2 3      + 6 1      + 2 6      + 4 2      + 1 1
 _____     _____     _____     _____     _____     _____
```

```
   2 5        6 2        3 2        2 5        8 2        9 1
 + 4 2      + 1 4      + 4 4      + 1 3      +   6      +   5
 _____     _____     _____     _____     _____     _____
```

Picture This

Add the ones, then the tens in each problem, Then, write the sum in the blank.

Example:

2 tens and 6 ones
+ 1 ten and 3 ones

3 tens and **9** ones = **39**

1 ten and 4 ones
+ 3 tens and 3 ones

___ tens and ___ ones = ___

2 tens and 5 ones
+ 2 tens and 3 ones

___ tens and ___ ones = ___

1 ten and 6 ones
+ 5 tens and 1 one

___ tens and ___ ones = ___

1 ten and 3 ones
+ 1 ten and 1 one

___ tens and ___ ones = ___

2 tens and 5 ones
+ 2 tens and 0 ones

___ tens and ___ ones = ___

1 ten and 5 ones
+ 2 tens and 4 ones

___ tens and ___ ones = ___

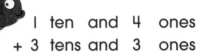

7 tens and 6 ones
+ 2 tens and 2 ones

___ tens and ___ ones = ___

Piling Up Points

Solve the addition problems below.

tens	ones
1	7
+ 2	1

tens	ones
3	4
+ 5	2

tens	ones
	5
+ 6	2

tens	ones
2	0
+ 4	0

tens	ones
5	1
+	8

tens	ones
7	2
+ 1	7

tens	ones
4	7
+ 2	1

tens	ones
2	5
+ 6	2

tens	ones
4	2
+ 2	4

tens	ones
8	3
+ 1	4

tens	ones
3	2
+ 2	5

Name _____

Circus Fun

Add to solve the problems.

tens	ones
2	5
+ 1	4

tens	ones
5	3
+ 3	2

tens	ones
7	1
+ 2	8

tens	ones
4	4
+ 3	2

tens	ones
5	1
+ 3	7

tens	ones
2	6
+ 5	2

tens	ones
2	6
+ 4	2

tens	ones
3	7
+ 5	1

tens	ones
1	9
+ 3	0

Fun with Tens and Ones

Add to find the sum.

tens	ones
3	5
+ 1	2

tens	ones
1	0
+ 3	2

tens	ones
5	4
+ 3	1

tens	ones
4	1
+ 3	6

tens	ones
3	5
+ 6	2

tens	ones
2	5
+ 2	2

tens	ones
4	1
+ 5	4

tens	ones
1	9
+ 4	0

Name ______________________________

Addition Challenge

Solve each problem.

Eileen walked 20 miles. ☐☐

Kathy walked 17 miles. + ☐☐

How many miles in all? ☐☐

Ken sees 25 mice. ☐☐

Pam sees 14 mice. + ☐☐

How many mice in all? ☐☐

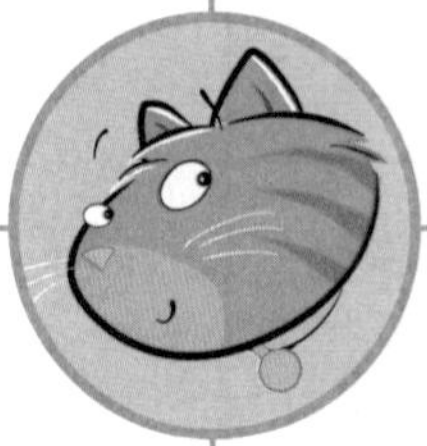

Ben sees 48 trees. ☐☐

Ron sees 41 trees. + ☐☐

How many trees in all? ☐☐

Oliver sleeps 22 hours. ☐☐

Clyde sleeps 11 hours. + ☐☐

How many hours in all? ☐☐

Name _____

Write the answers to each problem to find the number of bees in each hive.
Use the letters to solve the riddle.

K
26
+13

M
82
+15

L
12
+32

E
34
+45

J
92
+ 6

R
46
+31

B
61
+22

A
56
+12

C
70
+15

The honey was too hard to get, so Ted E. Bear ate
something else. What was it?

83	44	68	85	39

"   "

83	79	68	77	79		98	68	97

Add It Up!

Solve each problem.

Ken sees 25 birds.

Pilar sees 20 birds.　+

How many birds in all?

Rachel has 88 marbles.

Paul has 11 marbles.　+

How many marbles in all?

Sam has 11 rabbits.

Porchia has 25 rabbits.　+

How many rabbits in all?

Jorge has 53 coins.

Darrell has 36 coins.　+

How many coins in all?

Name _____

Scoreboard Sums

Add the total points scored in each game.

HOME	22
VISITOR	17

Total __**39**__

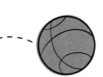

HOME	28
VISITOR	30

Total _____

HOME	55
VISITOR	21

Total _____

HOME	14
VISITOR	33

Total _____

HOME	24
VISITOR	13

Total _____

HOME	46
VISITOR	32

Total _____

HOME	83
VISITOR	06

Total _____

HOME	30
VISITOR	20

Total _____

HOME	17
VISITOR	42

Total _____

HOME	24
VISITOR	45

Total _____

Find the 10s

Circle the two numbers in each row that equal 10. Then, write the third number in the number sentence with 10 and solve for the sum. The first one has been done for you.

 12 + ⑨ + ① = 10 + __12__ = __22__

 7 + 26 + 3 = 10 + _____ = _____

 2 + 90 + 8 = 10 + _____ = _____

 5 + 86 + 5 = 10 + _____ = _____

 6 + 4 + 31 = 10 + _____ = _____

Find the 20s

Circle the two numbers in each row that equal 20. Then, write the third number in the number sentence with 20 and solve for the sum. The first one has been done for you.

$12 + (18) + (2)$ = $20 + \underline{12} = \underline{32}$

$17 + 26 + 3$ = $20 + \underline{} = \underline{}$

$8 + 80 + 12$ = $20 + \underline{} = \underline{}$

$10 + 97 + 10$ = $20 + \underline{} = \underline{}$

$14 + 6 + 41$ = $20 + \underline{} = \underline{}$

Add and Solve

Solve each problem.

Danny has 78 toys.

Yasmin has 21 toys.

$+$ ☐☐ / ☐☐

How many toys in all? ☐☐

Joanna has 11 puppies.

Pablo has 37 puppies.

$+$ ☐☐ / ☐☐

How many puppies in all? ☐☐

Rashawnda sees 38 clouds. ☐☐

Seth sees 41 clouds. ☐☐

$+$

How many clouds in all? ☐☐

Randy has 48 pretzels. ☐☐

Sierra has 51 pretzels. ☐☐

$+$

How many pretzels in all? ☐☐

Raccoon Roundup

Solve the addition problems. Write your answers inside the ropes.

$$\begin{array}{r} 26 \\ +43 \\ \hline \end{array}$$

$$\begin{array}{r} 34 \\ +10 \\ \hline \end{array}$$

$$\begin{array}{r} 57 \\ +20 \\ \hline \end{array}$$

$$\begin{array}{r} 43 \\ +55 \\ \hline \end{array}$$

$$\begin{array}{r} 43 \\ +31 \\ \hline \end{array}$$

$$\begin{array}{r} 48 \\ +20 \\ \hline \end{array}$$

$$\begin{array}{r} 52 \\ +34 \\ \hline \end{array}$$

$$\begin{array}{r} 67 \\ +22 \\ \hline \end{array}$$

Anchors Away

Solve the addition problems. Use the code to find the answer to this riddle:

What did the pirate have to do
before every trip out to sea?

48	36	58	96	69	75	89	29
O	H	G	B	T	E	N	A

42 +16	34 +41	60 + 9
58		
G		

17 +31	55 +34

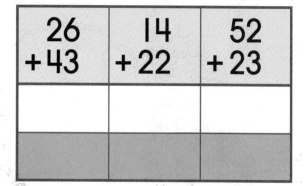

26 +43	14 +22	52 +23

83 +13	24 +24	5 +24	52 +17

Addition Challenge

Solve each problem.

Donna sees 38 cats.

Reba sees 61 cats.

$+$

How many cats in all?

Delinda has 10 ribbons.

Stefanie has 12 ribbons.

$+$

How many ribbons in all?

Chris has 29 pencils.

Bobbi has 40 pencils.

$+$

How many pencils in all?

Khalil sees 73 people.

Patrick sees 13 people.

$+$

How many people in all?

Addition Breakdown

Add each pair of numbers by breaking the second number into tens and ones. Then, add the groups of ten and add the ones. The first two have been started for you.

56 + 23 =

56 + 20 + 3 =

76 + 3 =

_____

28 + 14 =

28 + 10 + 4 =

_____ + _____ =

_____

46 + 39 =

_____ + _____ + _____ =

_____ + _____ =

_____

32 + 17 =

_____ + _____ + _____ =

_____ + _____ =

_____

Addition Breakdown

Add each pair of numbers by breaking the second number into tens and ones. Then, add the groups of ten and add the ones. The first two have been started for you.

57 + 33 =

57 + 30 + 3 =

87 + 3 =

_____

25 + 13 =

25 + 10 + 3 =

_____ + _____ =

_____

48 + 34 =

_____ + _____ + _____ =

_____ + _____ =

_____

37 + 18 =

_____ + _____ + _____ =

_____ + _____ =

_____

Brain Power

Use mental math to find each sum. (Hint: Make tens or multiples of 10 first.) Then, write in the cloud how you solved each problem.

12 + 5 + 8 + 5 =

31 + 7 + 3 =

7 + 9 + 13 =

80 + 19 + 1 =

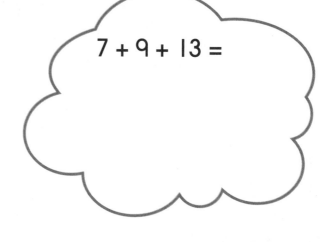

I BET YOU'LL BE ABLE TO FIGURE THIS OUT!

Brain Boost

Use mental math to find each sum. Then, write in the cloud how you solved each problem.

$41 + 8 + 2 =$

$13 + 4 + 7 + 4 =$

SHOW ME HOW IT'S DONE!

$70 + 18 + 3 =$

$8 + 7 + 14 =$

Add It Up!

Solve each problem.

Ruby has 39 candles.

Samir has 10 candles. +

How many candles in all?

Roberto sees 36 bugs.

Doug sees 32 bugs. +

How many bugs in all?

Myong ran 10 miles.

Dawn ran 13 miles. +

How many miles in all?

Greg has 31 bags.

Rudy has 48 bags. +

How many bags in all?

Time to Regroup

Addition is "putting together" or adding two or more numbers to find the sum. Regrouping is using ten ones to form one ten, ten tens to form one 100, fifteen ones to form one ten and five ones, and so on.

Study the examples. Follow the steps to add.

Example: 1 4
           + 8
           ‾‾‾‾‾

Step 1:
Add the ones.

tens	ones
1	4
+	8
	12

Step 2:
Regroup the tens.

tens	ones
1	
1	4
+	8
	2

Step 3:
Add the tens

tens	ones
1	
1	4
+	8
2	**2**

```
  2 8          3 2          5 4
+ 1 7        + 3 8        + 2 9
```

```
  1 9          4 4          2 5
+ 5 5        + 4 8        + 6 6
```

Nutty Action

Sam Squirrel and his friend Wendy were gathering acorns. When they gathered 10 acorns, they put them in a basket. The picture shows how many acorns Sam and Wendy each gathered. Write the numbers that tell how many.

How many acorns did Sam and Wendy gather in all?_____

Add these numbers. Regroup as needed.

tens	ones
3	8
+ 4	6

tens	ones
5	4
+ 2	7

tens	ones
4	9
+ 1	3

tens	ones
2	6
+ 1	7

Squirrelly Fun

Add to find the sum. Regroup as needed. Match the squirrels to their trees.

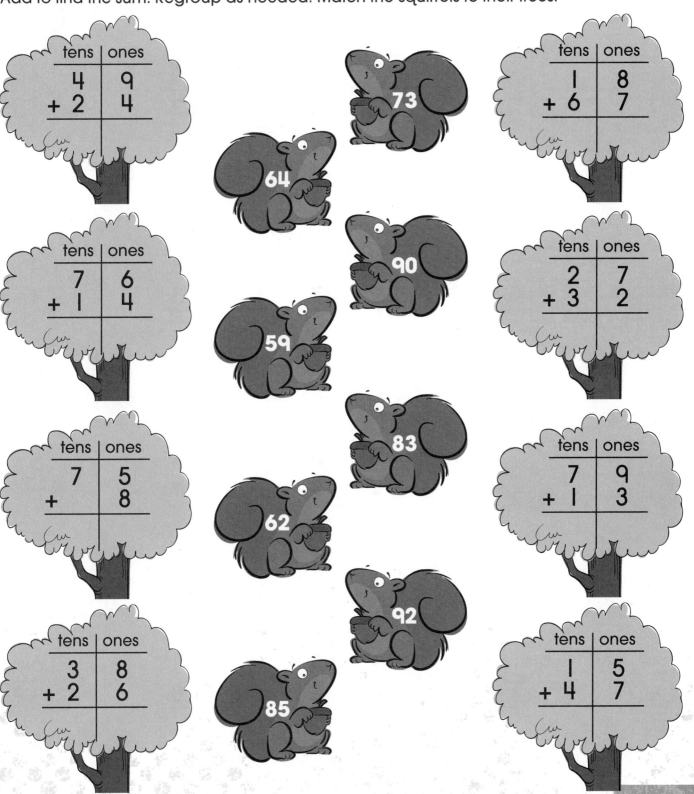

tens	ones
4	9
+ 2	4

73

tens	ones
1	8
+ 6	7

64

tens	ones
7	6
+ 1	4

90

tens	ones
2	7
+ 3	2

59

tens	ones
7	5
+	8

83

tens	ones
7	9
+ 1	3

62

92

tens	ones
3	8
+ 2	6

85

tens	ones
1	5
+ 4	7

Two-Digit Addition

Solve the problems.

```
    17        26        47        68        37
+   34    +   47    +   35    +   24    +   28


    29        58        69        78        19
+   48    +   27    +   17    +   13    +   44


    55        27        39        57        38
+   28    +   35    +   52    +   27    +   36


    49        65        23        64        46
+   43    +   18    +   18    +   18    +   39
```

Solve the Problems!

Solve each problem.

Example:

16 boys ride their bikes to school.

18 girls ride their bikes to school.

How many bikes are ridden to school?

$$\begin{array}{r} 1 \\ 1\,6 \\ +\,1\,8 \\ \hline 3\,4 \end{array}$$

Davis reads 26 pages.

Mike reads 37 pages.

How many pages did Davis and Mike read?

Travon counts 46 stars.

Nina counts 39 stars.

How many stars did they count?

Mom has 29 golf balls.

Dad has 43 golf balls.

How many golf balls do they have?

Shoot for the Stars

Add the total points scored in the game.

HOME	47
VISITOR	38

Total **85**

HOME	33
VISITOR	57

Total _____

HOME	43
VISITOR	49

Total _____

HOME	57
VISITOR	34

Total _____

HOME	29
VISITOR	22

Total _____

HOME	36
VISITOR	58

Total _____

HOME	45
VISITOR	39

Total _____

HOME	66
VISITOR	26

Total _____

HOME	72
VISITOR	19

Total _____

HOME	54
VISITOR	26

Total _____

Name _____

Keep on Truckin'

Write each sum. Connect the sums of 83 to make a road for the truck.

$$\begin{array}{r} 17 \\ + 66 \\ \hline \end{array} \qquad \begin{array}{r} 48 \\ + 26 \\ \hline \end{array} \qquad \begin{array}{r} 45 \\ + 19 \\ \hline \end{array}$$

$$\begin{array}{r} 28 \\ + 38 \\ \hline \end{array} \quad \begin{array}{r} 64 \\ + 19 \\ \hline \end{array} \quad \begin{array}{r} 26 \\ + 57 \\ \hline \end{array} \quad \begin{array}{r} 58 \\ + 25 \\ \hline \end{array} \quad \begin{array}{r} 17 \\ + 75 \\ \hline \end{array} \quad \begin{array}{r} 65 \\ + 29 \\ \hline \end{array}$$

$$\begin{array}{r} 37 \\ + 29 \\ \hline \end{array} \quad \begin{array}{r} 48 \\ + 35 \\ \hline \end{array} \quad \begin{array}{r} 58 \\ + 37 \\ \hline \end{array} \quad \begin{array}{r} 65 \\ + 16 \\ \hline \end{array} \quad \begin{array}{r} 38 \\ + 25 \\ \hline \end{array} \quad \begin{array}{r} 39 \\ + 59 \\ \hline \end{array}$$

$$\begin{array}{r} 59 \\ + 27 \\ \hline \end{array} \quad \begin{array}{r} 55 \\ + 28 \\ \hline \end{array} \quad \begin{array}{r} 39 \\ + 44 \\ \hline \end{array}$$

Brainy Book of Addition and Subtraction

Addition Challenge

Solve each problem.

Elijah has 29 hats.

Arifa has 52 hats.

+ ▢▢

How many hats in all?

Clarke has 73 cards.

Mandy has 25 cards.

+ ▢▢

How many cards in all?

Ryan sees 14 kites.

Alexa sees 48 kites.

+ ▢▢

How many kites in all?

Paige sees 14 bikes.

Ben sees 39 bikes.

+ ▢▢

How many bikes in all?

Just Like Magic

Add to find the sum.

A
```
  2 5
+ 4 9
```

I
```
  5 4
+ 2 6
```

E
```
  1 6
+ 1 8
```

R
```
  3 6
+ 1 9
```

O
```
  5 8
+ 1 7
```

W
```
  6 2
+ 2 9
```

Y
```
  2 8
+ 3 7
```

S
```
  2 9
+ 3 2
```

M
```
  4 6
+ 2 5
```

T
```
  1 8
+ 3 5
```

U
```
  3 8
+ 1 2
```

L
```
  3 9
+ 4 9
```

H
```
  4 7
+ 2 9
```

C
```
  6 9
+ 2 7
```

Use the answers and the letter on each lamp to solve the code.

71	74	65		74	88	88		65	75	50	55

91	80	61	76	34	61		96	75	71	34

!

53	55	50	34

Subtraction 1, 2, 3

Practice writing the numbers and then subtract.

1 —————————————————

2 —————————————————

3 —————————————————

$$\begin{array}{r} 3 \\ -1 \\ \hline \end{array}$$

$$\begin{array}{r} 4 \\ -3 \\ \hline \end{array}$$

$$\begin{array}{r} 2 \\ -1 \\ \hline \end{array}$$

$$\begin{array}{r} 3 \\ -2 \\ \hline \end{array}$$

Bubbly Baths

Solve the subtraction sentences below. Write each answer on a rubber duck.

5 – 4

1 – 0

4 – 2

2 – 1

3 – 2

3 – 1

1 – 1

5 – 1

4 – 1

Take It Slow!

Solve the subtraction sentences below. Use the code to color the turtle.

Code:
2 — red
3 — blue
4 — yellow
5 — green

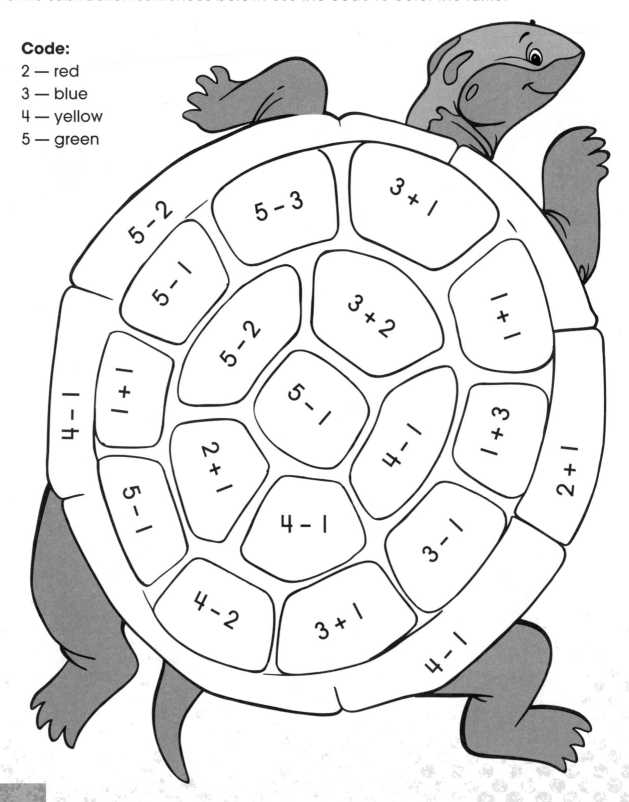

Squirrel Subtraction

Each squirrel ate some acorns. Cross out the number of acorns that each squirrel ate. Write how many acorns are left.

$5 - 3 =$ _____

$8 - 2 =$ _____

More Squirrel Subtraction

Each squirrel ate some acorns. Cross out the number of acorns that each squirrel ate. Write how many acorns are left.

$$7 - 4 = \underline{}$$

$$6 - 1 = \underline{}$$

Cat Chase!

Four hungry cats went on a picnic.

Two cats spotted some mice
and took off to catch them!

Solve the subtraction problem by answering the questions.

How many cats went on the picnic? _____

How many cats ran after the mice? _____

How many cats were left? _____

Name _____

Squirmy Worms

Solve the subtraction sentences below. Use the code to color the worms.

Code:

1 — red   2 — orange   3 — yellow   4 — brown

5 – 1 = ◯

3 – 2 = ◯

5 – 2 = ◯

3 – 1 = ◯

4 – 3 = ◯

5 – 3 = ◯
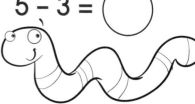

2 – 1 = ◯
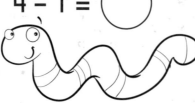

4 – 1 = ◯

5 – 1 = ◯

Subtraction 4, 5, 6

Practice writing the numbers and then subtract. Draw dots and cross them out, if needed.

4 -------------------------------

5 -------------------------------

6 -------------------------------

$$\begin{array}{r} 7 \\ -2 \\ \hline \end{array} \qquad \begin{array}{r} 6 \\ -1 \\ \hline \end{array}$$

$$\begin{array}{r} 6 \\ -2 \\ \hline \end{array} \qquad \begin{array}{r} 5 \\ -1 \\ \hline \end{array}$$

"Berry" Tasty

Solve the subtraction sentences below. Use the code to color the picture.

Code:

0 — green	2 — blue	4 — black
1 — brown	3 — purple	5 — pink

Making a Splash!

Six silly green frogs were
sitting on six lily pads.

A big bird flew by and two frogs
jumped off into the water.

Solve the subtraction problem by answering the questions.

How many frogs were sitting on the lily pads? _____

How many frogs jumped off? _____

How many frogs were left? _____

Nutty Subtraction

Count the nuts in each dish. Write the answer on the line by each dish.
Circle the problems that equal the answer.

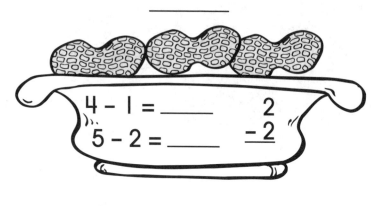

_____

$4 - 1 =$ _____   2
$5 - 2 =$ _____ -2

_____

$4 - 0 =$ _____   5
                      -2
$5 - 1 =$ _____

_____

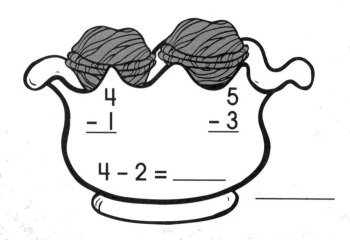

4   5
-1 -3

$4 - 2 =$ _____

_____

|

5
-2 $5 - 4 =$ |
3
        $3 - 2 =$ |

$5 - 0 =$ _____
5   2
-1 -2

_____

Name _____

Swamp Stories

Read the story. Subtract to find the difference. Write the number in the box.

Four alligators were in the water. One got out.
How many alligators were left in the water?

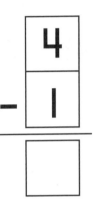

$$\begin{array}{r} 4 \\ -\ 1 \\ \hline \end{array}$$

Six frogs were sitting on lily pads. Two hopped away.
How many frogs were left on the lily pads?

$$\begin{array}{r} 6 \\ -\ 2 \\ \hline \end{array}$$

Five ducks were in the water. Three flew away.
How many ducks were left in the water?

$$\begin{array}{r} 5 \\ -\ 3 \\ \hline \end{array}$$

Brainy Book of Addition and Subtraction

111

Under the Sea

Complete the subtraction sentences.

How many 🐟's are left?

$$4 - 4 = \underline{\hspace{1.5cm}}$$

How many 🦭's are left?

$$6 - 2 = \underline{\hspace{1.5cm}}$$

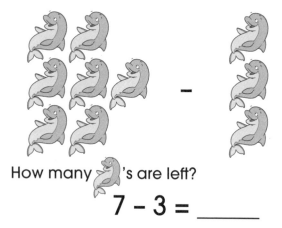

How many 🐬's are left?

$$7 - 3 = \underline{\hspace{1.5cm}}$$

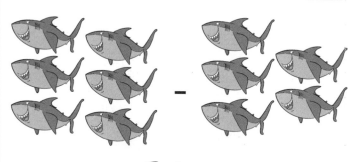
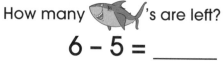

How many 🦈's are left?

$$6 - 5 = \underline{\hspace{1.5cm}}$$

How many 🐙's are left?

$$8 - 3 = \underline{\hspace{1.5cm}}$$

How many 🦭's are left?

$$5 - 2 = \underline{\hspace{1.5cm}}$$

Wheels and Wings

Complete the subtraction sentences.

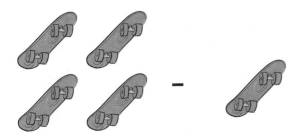

4 – 1 = _____

6 – 2 = _____

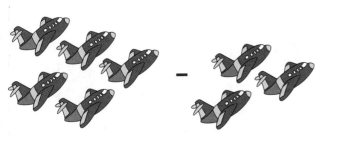

5 – 3 = _____

7 – 3 = _____

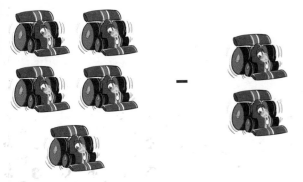

5 – 2 = _____

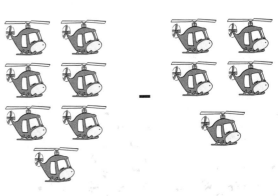

7 – 5 = _____

What's Left?

Complete the subtraction sentences.

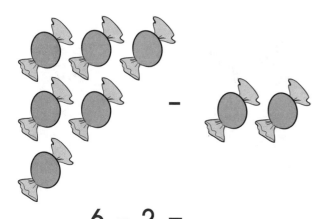

6 – 2 = _____

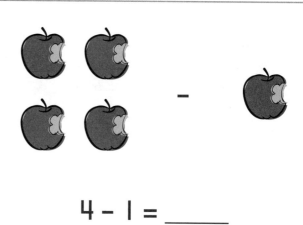

9 – 5 = _____

7 – 2 = _____

4 – 1 = _____

8 – 1 = _____

4 – 0 = _____

Take It Away!

Complete the subtraction sentences.

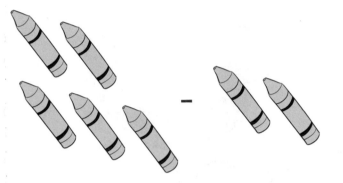

$$5 - 2 = \underline{\hspace{2em}}$$

$$6 - 1 = \underline{\hspace{2em}}$$

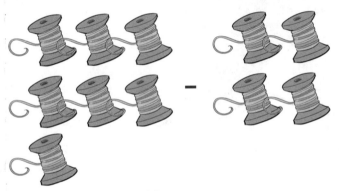

$$7 - 4 = \underline{\hspace{2em}}$$

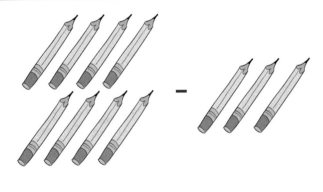

$$8 - 3 = \underline{\hspace{2em}}$$

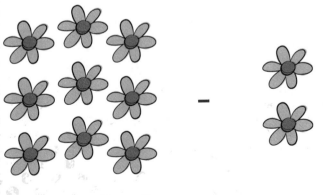

$$9 - 2 = \underline{\hspace{2em}}$$

$$4 - 4 = \underline{\hspace{2em}}$$

A Whale of a Job!

Use fish crackers to subtract. Put the number of fish needed in the "water." Then, take them away by sliding them into the whale's mouth. Count how many fish are left.

$$\begin{array}{r} 7 \\ -\ 3 \\ \hline \end{array}$$
$$\begin{array}{r} 9 \\ -\ 2 \\ \hline \end{array}$$
$$\begin{array}{r} 6 \\ -\ 4 \\ \hline \end{array}$$
$$\begin{array}{r} 5 \\ -\ 2 \\ \hline \end{array}$$
$$\begin{array}{r} 8 \\ -\ 3 \\ \hline \end{array}$$

$$\begin{array}{r} 9 \\ -\ 3 \\ \hline \end{array}$$
$$\begin{array}{r} 6 \\ -\ 3 \\ \hline \end{array}$$
$$\begin{array}{r} 7 \\ -\ 5 \\ \hline \end{array}$$
$$\begin{array}{r} 8 \\ -\ 2 \\ \hline \end{array}$$
$$\begin{array}{r} 5 \\ -\ 1 \\ \hline \end{array}$$

8 – 4 = _____   6 – 2 = _____   7 – 4 = _____

At the Bakery

Look at each number sentence. Find each missing number by circling the food items that are left over.

$$5 - \underline{} = 4$$

$$6 - \underline{} = 4$$

Bake and Take

Look at each number sentence. Find each missing number by circling the food items that are left over.

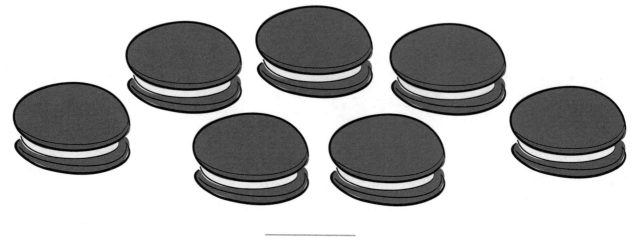

$$7 - \underline{\hspace{2cm}} = 3$$

$$8 - \underline{\hspace{2cm}} = 2$$

Hop Along!

Use the number line to count back.

Example: 8 - 3 = __5__   8, __7__ , __6__, __5__

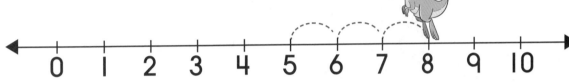

7 - 3 = ____

7,____,____,____

6 - 2 = ____

6,____,____

8 - 1 = ____

8,____

7 - 2 = ____

7,____,____

Too Many Toys!

Write the number sentence for each picture.

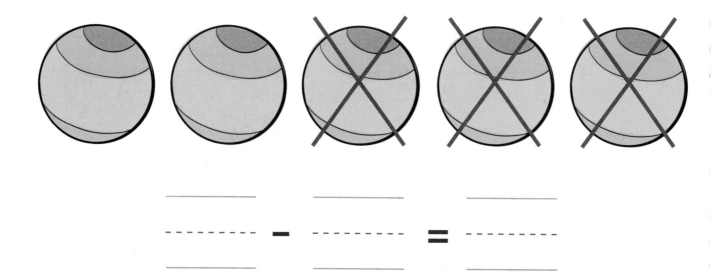

_____   _____   _____
- - - - - - ▬ - - - - - ▬ - - - - - -
_____   _____   _____

_____   _____   _____
- - - - - - ▬ - - - - - ▬ - - - - - -
_____   _____   _____

Toy Takeaway

Write the number sentence for each picture.

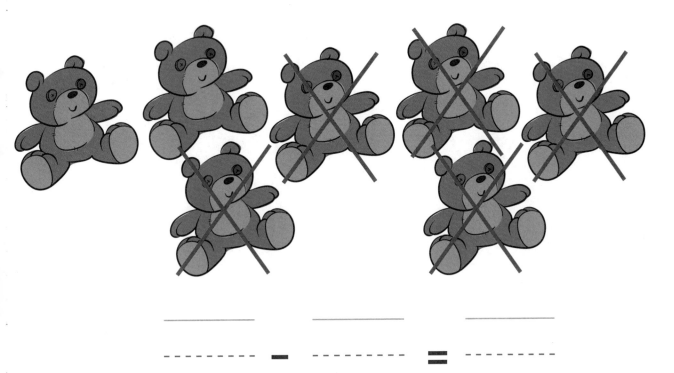

_____   _____   _____
- - - - - - ▬ - - - - - - ▬ - - - - - -
_____   _____   _____

_____   _____   _____
- - - - - - - - ▬ - - - - - - - ▬ - - - - - - -
_____   _____   _____

Blow the Horn!

Subtract by circling the horns.

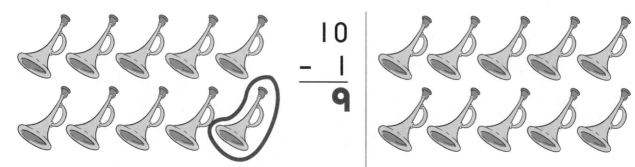

$$\begin{array}{r} 10 \\ - 1 \\ \hline 9 \end{array}$$

10 – 1 = __9__

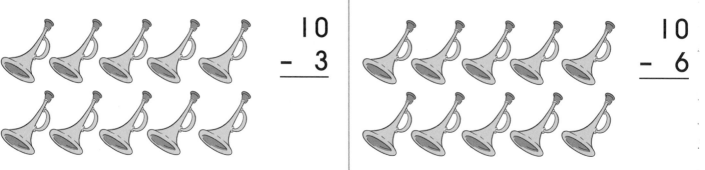

$$\begin{array}{r} 10 \\ - 9 \\ \hline \end{array}$$

10 – 9 = ____

$$\begin{array}{r} 10 \\ - 3 \\ \hline \end{array}$$

10 – 3 = ____

$$\begin{array}{r} 10 \\ - 6 \\ \hline \end{array}$$

10 – 6 = ____

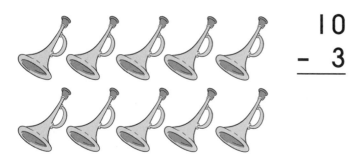

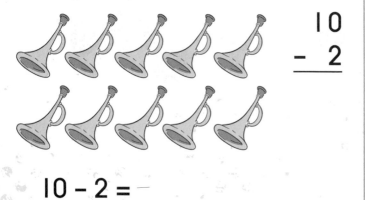

$$\begin{array}{r} 10 \\ - 2 \\ \hline \end{array}$$

10 – 2 = ____

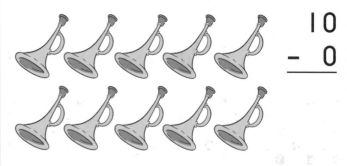

$$\begin{array}{r} 10 \\ - 0 \\ \hline \end{array}$$

10 – 0 = ____

What's the Difference?

Color the two numbers in each box that show the given difference.

Difference of 1

6	4
3	8

3	1
5	6

4	0
1	7

Difference of 1

3	7
1	8

2	3
5	7

6	3
9	7

Difference of 2

3	0
7	1

3	8
6	9

7	1
4	5

Difference of 2

3	4
8	2

7	4
10	5

10	8
5	4

Difference of 0

2	1
4	2

7	3
8	3

5	6
5	4

Number Neighbors

Circle the two numbers next to each other that make the given difference. Find as many as you can in each row.

Difference of 1

(2	3)	0	8	7	2	9	10	6	5	1	4	4	3

Difference of 1

8	4	5	3	7	1	2	4	9	8	0	1	7	6

Difference of 2

5	4	2	3	1	0	2	5	8	9	7	6	8	5

Difference of 2

7	5	10	8	1	4	6	3	1	6	7	9	2	0

Difference of 3

1	6	3	2	8	4	7	6	10	7	3	9	5	2

How Many Left?

Solve each problem.

There are 10 white .

There are four blue .

How many more white than blue are there? __**6**__

$$\begin{array}{r} 10 \\ -4 \\ \hline 6 \end{array}$$

Ten are on the table.

Two are broken.

How many are not broken? _____

There are nine .

Six swim away.

How many are left? _____

Joni wants nine .

She has five .

How many more does she need? _____

There were 10  .

Five melted.

How many did not melt? _____

Sweet Treats

Count the candy in each dish. Write the number on the line by each dish. Circle the problems that equal the answer.

10 – 1 = _____

10 – 4 = _____

9
– 1
____

7 – 1 = _____

8
– 2
____

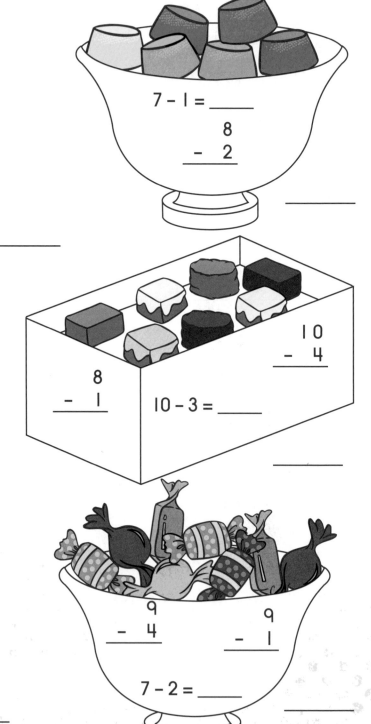

10
– 4
____

8
– 1
____

10 – 3 = _____

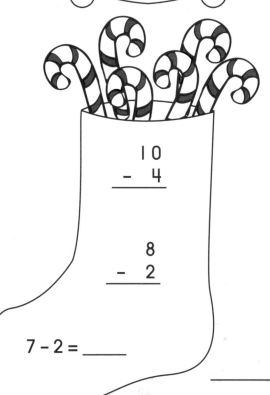

10
– 4
____

8
– 2
____

7 – 2 = _____

9
– 4
____

9
– 1
____

7 – 2 = _____

Name

Something Fishy

Solve the subtraction problems below.

5 − 3	6 − 1

4 − 3	3 − 1	2 − 0	1 − 1
9 − 2	7 − 4	10 − 5	8 − 6
7 − 2	6 − 3	10 − 2	8 − 3
6 − 4	5 − 2	9 − 6	4 − 1

Frogs on a Log

Roll a die. Starting at 10, count back the rolled number as hops on the log. Write what you did as a subtraction fact. Repeat four more times.

Secrets of Subtraction

Solve the subtraction problems. Use the code to find the secret message.

Code:

7	5	2	6	4	3
K	T	Y	E	W	A

PLEASE, DON'T EVER

8 − 3	10 − 7	9 − 2	10 − 4		9 − 6	6 − 2	7 − 4	8 − 6

___	___	___	___		___	___	___	___

MY MATH!

Chalk It Up!

Solve the subtraction problems below.

10	7	6	4	3
− 5	− 2	− 3	− 3	− 2

8	10	7	10	10
− 6	− 7	− 1	− 1	− 5

2	6	8	9	8	9	10
− 1	− 4	− 4	− 5	− 1	− 2	− 3

8	9	5	10	7	4	6
− 7	− 6	− 4	− 6	− 3	− 2	− 2

10	5	9	9	8	7	6
− 8	− 1	− 5	− 3	− 5	− 3	− 4

Count the crayons. Write the number on the blank. Circle the problems that equal the answer.

_____ II

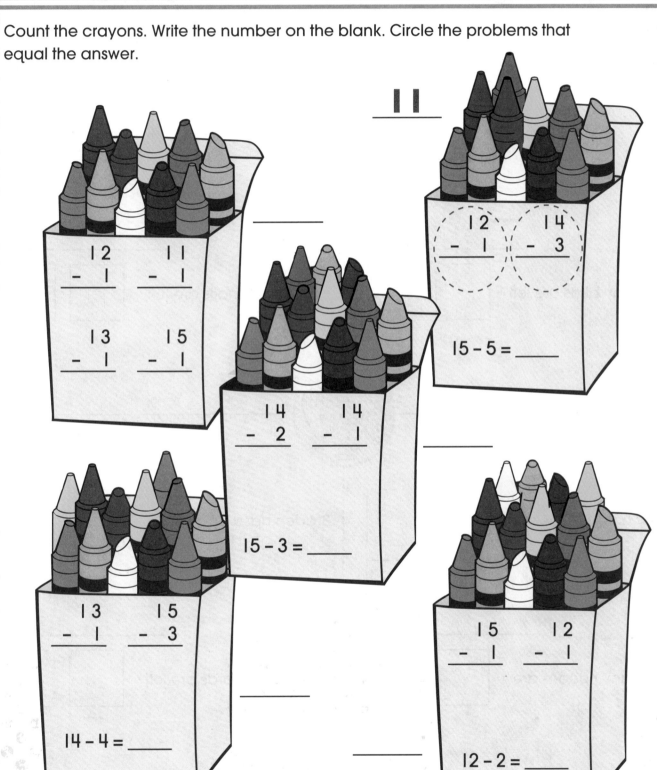

_____

$$\begin{array}{cc} 12 & 11 \\ -\ 1 & -\ 1 \end{array}$$

$$\begin{array}{cc} 13 & 15 \\ -\ 1 & -\ 1 \end{array}$$

$$\begin{array}{cc} 12 & 14 \\ -\ 1 & -\ 3 \end{array}$$

$$15 - 5 = \rule{1cm}{0.4pt}$$

$$\begin{array}{cc} 14 & 14 \\ -\ 2 & -\ 1 \end{array}$$

$$15 - 3 = \rule{1cm}{0.4pt}$$

$$\begin{array}{cc} 13 & 15 \\ -\ 1 & -\ 3 \end{array}$$

_____

$$14 - 4 = \rule{1cm}{0.4pt}$$

$$\begin{array}{cc} 15 & 12 \\ -\ 1 & -\ 1 \end{array}$$

_____

$$12 - 2 = \rule{1cm}{0.4pt}$$

Subtraction Challenge

Solve each problem.

Kenyon sees 18 birds.

3 fly away.

How many birds are left?

Carlos sees 19 snails.

Trey takes 6 snails.

How many snails are left?

Kelsey has 18 ribbons.

She loses 7 ribbons.

How many ribbons are left?

Braden has 17 cards.

He gives 2 away.

How many cards are left?

Fun Facts

Solve the subtraction problems below.

```
  16          14          17
-  9        -  7        -  9


  14          15          16          12
-  8        -  8        -  8        -  3


  14          18          15          13
-  9        -  9        -  9        -  7


  16          15          13          12
-  8        -  8        -  8        -  4


  14          13          16          13
-  6        -  3        -  7        -  9
```

How Many Are Left?

Solve each problem.

Taylor has 19 kites.

She gives 7 away.

How many kites are left?

Spencer has 14 pencils.

1 pencil breaks.

How many pencils are left?

Lily has 18 shoes.

Her sister takes 2 shoes.

How many shoes are left?

Colby draws 18 pictures.

He erases 7 pictures.

How many pictures are left?

Three in a Row

Solve each subtraction problem. Then, draw a line to connect the three answers in each row that are the same.

12 – 9 =	11 – 2 =	9 – 8 =
_____	_____	_____
8 – 6 =	7 – 4 =	7 – 5 =
_____	_____	_____
7 – 3 =	10 – 1 =	11 – 8 =
_____	_____	_____

10 – 7 =	12 – 3 =	11 – 2 =
_____	_____	_____
12 – 7 =	9 – 0 =	8 – 5 =
_____	_____	_____
11 – 4 =	9 – 2 =	12 – 5 =
_____	_____	_____

9 – 7 =	11 – 9 =	10 – 2 =
_____	_____	_____
11 – 5 =	9 – 3 =	12 – 6 =
_____	_____	_____
8 – 1 =	12 – 7 =	9 – 5 =
_____	_____	_____

7 – 7 =	11 – 6 =	9 – 1 =
_____	_____	_____
10 – 3 =	9 – 4 =	10 – 0 =
_____	_____	_____
8 – 8 =	10 – 5 =	12 – 4 =
_____	_____	_____

Subtract and Solve

Solve each problem.

Chelsea sees 16 planes.

7 planes take off.

How many planes are left?

Sam has 17 marbles.

He loses 8 at school.

How many marbles are left?

Ella has 12 cookies.

Her brother takes 4 cookies.

How many cookies are left?

Yuri buys 18 pencils.

He gives away 9 pencils.

How many pencils are left?

Play Ball!

Solve the problems.

Example:

$$13 - 5 = \mathbf{8}$$

$$14 - 9$$

$$14 - 8$$

$$13 - 4$$

$$12 - 7$$ $$10 - 2$$ $$13 - 4$$ $$14 - 9$$ $$11 - 8$$ $$14 - 5$$

$$14 - 6$$ $$12 - 8$$ $$13 - 5$$ $$10 - 6$$ $$13 - 6$$ $$13 - 7$$

$$11 - 6$$ $$13 - 9$$ $$14 - 8$$ $$12 - 3$$ $$14 - 7$$ $$13 - 8$$

School Subtraction

Solve the problems.

Example:

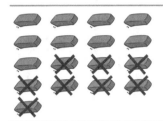

$$\begin{array}{r} 15 \\ -\ 7 \\ \hline \mathbf{8} \end{array}$$

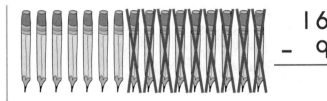

$$\begin{array}{r} 16 \\ -\ 9 \\ \hline \end{array}$$

$$\begin{array}{r} 17 \\ -\ 8 \\ \hline \end{array}$$

$$\begin{array}{r} 18 \\ -\ 9 \\ \hline \end{array}$$

$$\begin{array}{r} 18 \\ -\ 9 \\ \hline \end{array}$$
$$\begin{array}{r} 13 \\ -\ 5 \\ \hline \end{array}$$
$$\begin{array}{r} 16 \\ -\ 8 \\ \hline \end{array}$$
$$\begin{array}{r} 17 \\ -\ 9 \\ \hline \end{array}$$
$$\begin{array}{r} 14 \\ -\ 6 \\ \hline \end{array}$$
$$\begin{array}{r} 13 \\ -\ 9 \\ \hline \end{array}$$

$$\begin{array}{r} 17 \\ -\ 8 \\ \hline \end{array}$$
$$\begin{array}{r} 15 \\ -\ 9 \\ \hline \end{array}$$
$$\begin{array}{r} 14 \\ -\ 5 \\ \hline \end{array}$$
$$\begin{array}{r} 13 \\ -\ 6 \\ \hline \end{array}$$
$$\begin{array}{r} 16 \\ -\ 7 \\ \hline \end{array}$$
$$\begin{array}{r} 12 \\ -\ 4 \\ \hline \end{array}$$

$$\begin{array}{r} 14 \\ -\ 7 \\ \hline \end{array}$$
$$\begin{array}{r} 15 \\ -\ 8 \\ \hline \end{array}$$
$$\begin{array}{r} 16 \\ -\ 9 \\ \hline \end{array}$$
$$\begin{array}{r} 12 \\ -\ 7 \\ \hline \end{array}$$
$$\begin{array}{r} 15 \\ -\ 7 \\ \hline \end{array}$$
$$\begin{array}{r} 13 \\ -\ 4 \\ \hline \end{array}$$

Subtraction Challenge

Solve each problem.

Zach sees 17 cars.

4 cars drive away. ──

How many cars are left?

Samaria sees 19 leaves.

9 blow away. ──

How many leaves are left?

Virginia has 18 dollars.

She spends 5 dollars. ──

How many dollars
are left?

Ramsey sees 16 boats.

3 boats leave. ──

How many boats are left?

How Many More?

Count the gumballs in the pair of gumball machines. Write a number sentence to show how many more gumballs are in the first machine.

_____ — _____ = _____

Gumballs Galore

Count the gumballs in the pair of gumball machines. Write a number sentence to show how many more gumballs are in the first machine.

_____   _____   _____

- - - - - - - **-** - - - - - - - **=** - - - - - - -

Subtract and Solve

Solve each problem.

Gerardo mows 15 lawns. ☐ ☐

He finished 2 lawns. — ☐

How many lawns are left? ☐ ☐

Devon can swim 19 laps. ☐ ☐

She has swum 2 laps. — ☐

How many laps are left? ☐ ☐

Dan's house is 19 miles away. ☐ ☐

He has driven 8 miles. — ☐

How many miles are left? ☐ ☐

Leigh writes 15 letters. ☐ ☐

She sends out 1 letter. — ☐

How many letters are left? ☐ ☐

Brainy Book of Addition and Subtraction

Wrong Hats

Draw an X on each dog with the wrong answer. Find 6 wrong answers.

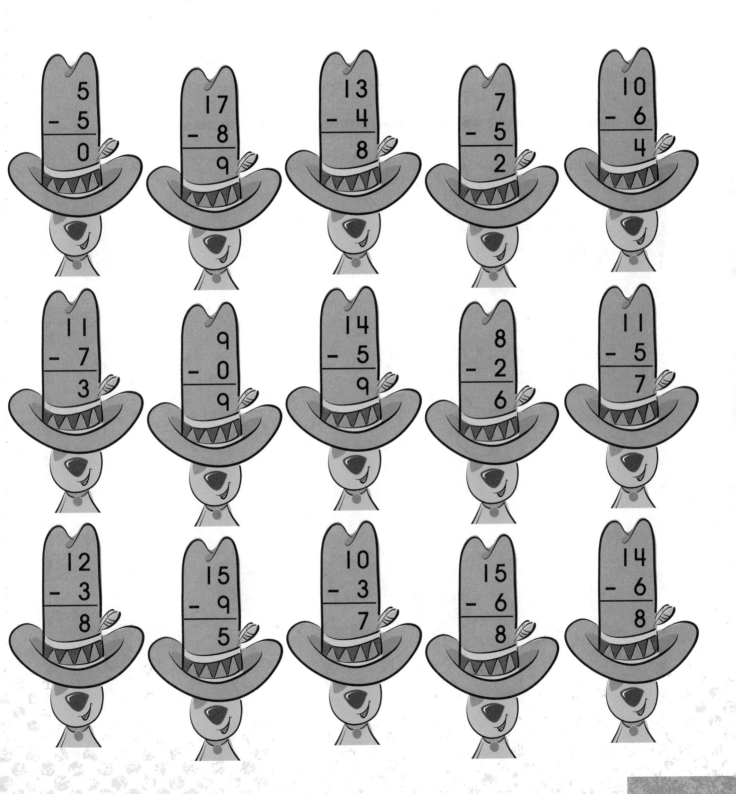

Big Cat!

Subtract. Write the answer in the space. Then, color the spaces according to the answers.

Code:

1 — white	2 — purple	3 — black	4 — green	5 — yellow
6 — blue	7 — pink	8 — gray	9 — orange	10 — red

Stop and Subtract

Solve each problem.

Leo sees 16 pennies. ☐ ☐

He picks up 6 pennies. ─── ☐

How many pennies are left? ☐ ☐

Molly sees 18 cats. ☐ ☐

2 cats run away. ─── ☐

How many cats are left? ☐ ☐

Alfonso catches 16 fish. ☐ ☐

Shelby catches 4 fish. ─── ☐

Alfonso has how many more fish? ☐ ☐

Jill has 13 presents. ☐ ☐

She gives 2 away. ─── ☐

How many presents are left? ☐ ☐

Monster Marbles

Solve the problems.

Once there was a monster named Miles who spent every day playing marbles. He kept his 20 favorite marbles in a beautiful marble bag. One day, he grabbed his marbles and went to play with his friends.

At Wayne's house, he lost 10 marbles. How many marbles did he have left?

$$20 - 10 = \underline{\hspace{2cm}}$$

At Rosa's house, he lost two more! Carry down the total to the next blank.

$$\underline{\hspace{2cm}} - 2 = \underline{\hspace{2cm}}$$

At Mohammed's house, he lost three more!

$$\underline{\hspace{2cm}} - 3 = \underline{\hspace{2cm}}$$

At Nikki's house, he lost four more!

$$\underline{\hspace{2cm}} - 4 = \underline{\hspace{2cm}}$$

What a sad day for Miles!
How many marbles did he have left? _____

How Many Animals Are Left?

Write a number sentence to solve each subtraction problem.

1. Lamonte had 10 kittens, but 4 of them ran away. How many kittens does he have left?

_____

2. There were 12 rabbits eating in the garden. Dogs chased 3 of them away. How many rabbits were left?

_____

3. There were 14 frogs on the bank of the pond. Then, 9 of them hopped into the water. How many frogs were left on the bank?

_____

4. Kennedy saw 11 birds eating from the bird feeders in her backyard. A cat scared 7 of them away. How many birds were left at the feeders?

_____

5. Felipe counted 15 robins in his yard. Then, 8 of the robins flew away. How many robins were left in the yard?

_____

Subtraction Challenge

Solve each problem.

Maricela has 17 balloons. ☐ ☐

9 balloons fly away. — ☐

How many balloons are left? ☐

Renee sees 15 cars. ☐ ☐

1 car drives away. — ☐

How many cars are left? ☐ ☐

Jasper has 14 pens. ☐ ☐

He loses 4 pens. — ☐

How many pens are left? ☐ ☐

Kade sees 18 birds. ☐ ☐

9 birds fly away. — ☐

How many birds are left? ☐

Subtraction Squares

Subtract each row and then each column. Write the answers on the lines.

| 11 | 6 | ---- |
3	2	----

| 14 | 7 | ---- |
5	4	----

| 16 | 8 | ---- |
9	4	----

Subtraction Squares

Subtract each row and then each column. Write the answers on the lines.

10	4	- - - - - -
3	2	- - - - - -
_____	_____	_____

13	8	- - - - - -
5	4	- - - - - -
_____	_____	_____

15	7	- - - - - -
9	4	- - - - - -
_____	_____	_____

Flower Power

Subtract to find the difference.

6 − 3	11 − 4	15 − 6	11 − 6

12 − 3	10 − 6	12 − 4	10 − 5	13 − 5	8 − 7	12 − 3

14 − 8	17 − 9	8 − 4	15 − 7	14 − 9	10 − 3	13 − 4

9 − 6	12 − 9	14 − 6	8 − 5	12 − 7	18 − 9	14 − 6

8 − 5	12 − 7	18 − 9	14 − 6	13 − 8	13 − 6	17 − 8

Subtract and Solve

Solve each problem.

Emily sees 12 flies.

6 flies fly away. —

How many flies are left?

Erin has 15 watches.

3 watches break. —

How many watches are left?

Dave sees 13 clouds.

3 clouds drift away. —

How many clouds are left?

Corey has 17 cards.

He keeps them all. —

How many cards are left?

Going "Batty"!

Subtract to find the difference.

```
  11      12      13       9
-  9    -  6    -  9    -  4
_____   _____   _____   _____
```

```
  14      14       8      11      17      11      13
-  9    -  7    -  5    -  2    -  1    -  5    -  5
_____   _____   _____   _____   _____   _____   _____
```

```
  15      13       8      14      16      10       8
-  6    -  4    -  4    -  6    -  7    -  6    -  3
_____   _____   _____   _____   _____   _____   _____
```

```
   9      18      14      10      14      15      11
-  5    -  9    -  6    -  3    -  8    -  8    -  8
_____   _____   _____   _____   _____   _____   _____
```

```
  11      14      13       5      12       7      16
-  3    -  4    -  7    -  2    -  5    -  4    -  8
_____   _____   _____   _____   _____   _____   _____
```

Subtraction Challenge

Solve each problem.

Ronaldo has 13 bikes.

He gives 5 to his friends.

How many bikes are left?

Gabe has 15 peas.

He eats 9 peas.

How many peas are left?

Lindsay has 11 dollars.

She spends 6 dollars.

How many dollars are left?

Brianna sees 18 planes.

7 planes take off.

How many planes are left?

Two-Digit Subtraction

Look at the example. Follow the steps to subtract.

Example:

```
   2 8
 - 1 4
 ─────
   1 4
```

Step 1: Subtract the ones.

tens	ones
2	8
– 1	4
	4

Step 2: Subtract the tens.

tens	ones
2	8
– 1	4
1	4

```
   2 4          6 1          7 7
 - 1 2        - 3 0        - 4 4
```

```
   8 5          5 7          8 7
 - 2 4        - 2 3        - 3 3
```

All Aboard!

Count the tens and ones and write the numbers. Then, subtract to solve the problems.

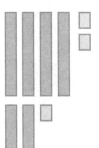

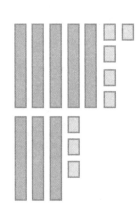

tens	ones
4	2
2	1

tens	ones

tens	ones

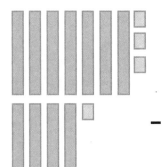

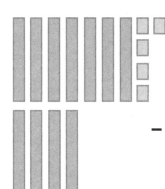

tens	ones

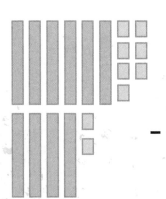

tens	ones

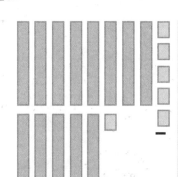

tens	ones

Brainy Book of Addition and Subtraction

Cookie Mania

There are 46 cookies. Bill eats 22 cookies.
How many are left?

$$\begin{array}{r} 46 \\ -22 \\ \hline \end{array}$$

Step 1: Subtract the ones.

tens	ones
4	6
- 2	2
	4

Step 2: Subtract the tens.

tens	ones
4	6
- 2	2
2	4

Subtract the ones first. Then, subtract the tens.

tens	ones
7	8
- 2	5

tens	ones
5	9
- 3	6

tens	ones
8	3
- 6	1

tens	ones
6	7
- 4	3

tens	ones
4	7
- 1	4

tens	ones
5	4
- 3	0

tens	ones
4	2
- 3	1

tens	ones
2	8
- 1	8

Subtraction Challenge

Solve each problem.

Ahmet baked 58 cookies. ☐ ☐

Cara eats 16 cookies. — ☐ ☐

How many are left? ☐ ☐

Penny sees 34 dogs. ☐ ☐

19 dogs run away. — ☐ ☐

How many are left? ☐ ☐

Alicia has 87 tickets. ☐ ☐

She sells 15 tickets. — ☐ ☐

How many tickets are left? ☐ ☐

Marc rents 25 movies. ☐ ☐

He returns 14 movies. — ☐ ☐

How many movies are left? ☐ ☐

Name _____

Subtract and Solve

Solve each problem.

Abel sees 25 birds.

20 birds fly away.

How many birds are left?

Shane has 74 marbles.

Ulric takes 43 marbles.

How many marbles are left?

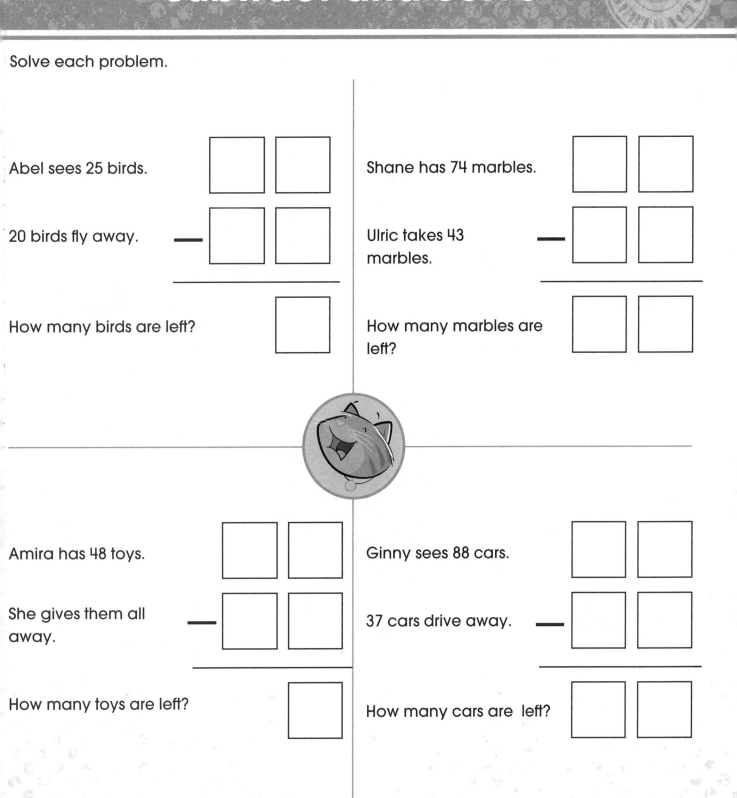

Amira has 48 toys.

She gives them all away.

How many toys are left?

Ginny sees 88 cars.

37 cars drive away.

How many cars are left?

Warm Up!

The players warm up before each game. Subtract to find out how many of each exercise the coach wants the players to do.

$$\begin{array}{r} 38 \\ -13 \\ \hline \end{array}$$
sit-ups

$$\begin{array}{r} 50 \\ -20 \\ \hline \end{array}$$
jumping jacks

$$\begin{array}{r} 17 \\ -7 \\ \hline \end{array}$$
sprints

$$\begin{array}{r} 69 \\ -33 \\ \hline \end{array}$$
toe touches

$$\begin{array}{r} 89 \\ -74 \\ \hline \end{array}$$
crunches

$$\begin{array}{r} 92 \\ -20 \\ \hline \end{array}$$
push-ups

How Many Are Left?

Solve the problems.

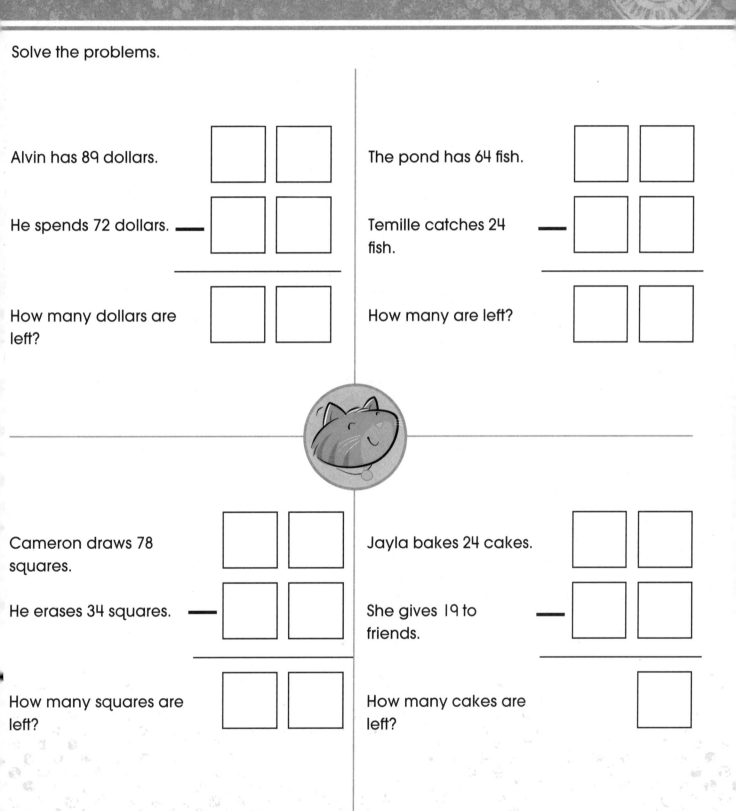

Alvin has 89 dollars.

He spends 72 dollars. —

How many dollars are left?

The pond has 64 fish.

Temille catches 24 fish. —

How many are left?

Cameron draws 78 squares.

He erases 34 squares. —

How many squares are left?

Jayla bakes 24 cakes.

She gives 19 to friends. —

How many cakes are left?

Mystery Numbers

Find the missing number behind each magnifying lens. Write a number sentence to solve for the missing number. Then, write the answer.

$77 - \bigcirc = 70$

_____ ☐ _____ = _____

$\bigcirc = $ _____

$29 - \bigcirc = 17$

_____ ☐ _____ = _____

$\bigcirc = $ _____

Digit Detective

Find the missing number behind each magnifying lens. Write a number sentence to solve for the missing number. Then, write the answer.

$21 - \underline{\hspace{1cm}} = 10$

$\underline{\hspace{1.5cm}} \ \Box \ \underline{\hspace{1.5cm}} = \underline{\hspace{1.5cm}}$

$\underline{\hspace{1cm}} = \underline{\hspace{1.5cm}}$

$37 - \underline{\hspace{1cm}} = 15$

$\underline{\hspace{1.5cm}} \ \Box \ \underline{\hspace{1.5cm}} = \underline{\hspace{1.5cm}}$

$\underline{\hspace{1cm}} = \underline{\hspace{1.5cm}}$

Subtraction Challenge

Solve each problem.

Lonnie sees 68 bugs. ☐ ☐

52 bugs crawl away. — ☐ ☐

How many bugs are left? ☐ ☐

Myra writes 95 letters. ☐ ☐

She sends out 74 letters. — ☐ ☐

How many letters are left? ☐ ☐

Jaime's house is 78 miles away. ☐ ☐

She has gone 63 miles. — ☐ ☐

How many miles are left? ☐ ☐

Andre has 24 papers. ☐ ☐

He delivers 12. — ☐ ☐

How many papers are left? ☐ ☐

Lion's Lunch

Leon the Lion was very hungry.
Write the answers to the problems
to find out how many bones he ate.
Circle all the differences that are
smaller than 20.

$$\begin{array}{r} 56 \\ -42 \\ \hline \end{array} \qquad \begin{array}{r} 39 \\ -18 \\ \hline \end{array} \qquad \begin{array}{r} 44 \\ -21 \\ \hline \end{array} \qquad \begin{array}{r} 26 \\ -13 \\ \hline \end{array} \qquad \begin{array}{r} 67 \\ -35 \\ \hline \end{array}$$

$$\begin{array}{r} 88 \\ -15 \\ \hline \end{array} \qquad \begin{array}{r} 79 \\ -58 \\ \hline \end{array} \qquad \begin{array}{r} 59 \\ -28 \\ \hline \end{array} \qquad \begin{array}{r} 68 \\ -47 \\ \hline \end{array} \qquad \begin{array}{r} 94 \\ -83 \\ \hline \end{array}$$

$$\begin{array}{r} 32 \\ -21 \\ \hline \end{array} \qquad \begin{array}{r} 56 \\ -15 \\ \hline \end{array} \qquad \begin{array}{r} 86 \\ -23 \\ \hline \end{array} \qquad \begin{array}{r} 74 \\ -31 \\ \hline \end{array} \qquad \begin{array}{r} 66 \\ -52 \\ \hline \end{array}$$

Cookie Craze!

Subtract to solve the problems. Circle the answers. Color the cookies with answers greater than 30.

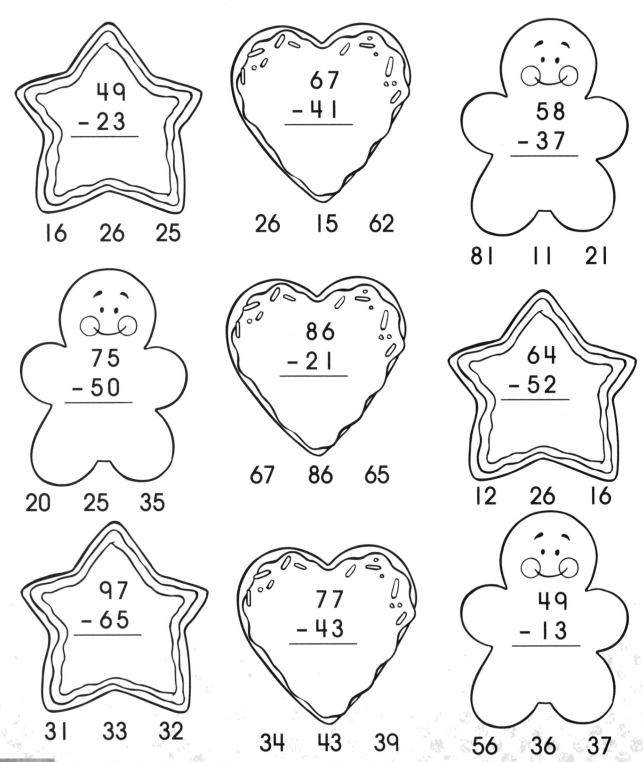

$$\begin{array}{r} 49 \\ -23 \\ \hline \end{array}$$

16   26   25

$$\begin{array}{r} 67 \\ -41 \\ \hline \end{array}$$

26   15   62

$$\begin{array}{r} 58 \\ -37 \\ \hline \end{array}$$

81   11   21

$$\begin{array}{r} 75 \\ -50 \\ \hline \end{array}$$

20   25   35

$$\begin{array}{r} 86 \\ -21 \\ \hline \end{array}$$

67   86   65

$$\begin{array}{r} 64 \\ -52 \\ \hline \end{array}$$

12   26   16

$$\begin{array}{r} 97 \\ -65 \\ \hline \end{array}$$

31   33   32

$$\begin{array}{r} 77 \\ -43 \\ \hline \end{array}$$

34   43   39

$$\begin{array}{r} 49 \\ -13 \\ \hline \end{array}$$

56   36   37

How Many Are Left?

Solve each problem.

Javon has 59 books.   ☐ ☐

He gives 32 away.   — ☐ ☐

How many books are left?   ☐ ☐

Rebecca has 87 marbles.   ☐ ☐

She loses 33 marbles.   — ☐ ☐

How many marbles are left?   ☐ ☐

Ana sees 70 leaves.   ☐ ☐

68 leaves blow away.   — ☐ ☐

How many leaves are left?   ☐

Blake sees 69 bees.   ☐ ☐

12 bees fly away.   — ☐ ☐

How many bees are left?   ☐ ☐

Take the Shortcut

Use the shortcuts to find each difference.

- 8 Shortcut	- 9 Shortcut
Think: −10, +2	Think: −10, +1

14 - 8 _____ − 10 + 2 = _____

30 - 9 _____ − 10 + 1 = _____

20 - 8 _____ − 10 + ___ = _____

40 - 9 _____ − 10 + ___ = _____

Use the shortcuts to find each difference.

| **– 8 Shortcut** Think: –10, +2 | **– 9 Shortcut** Think: –10, +1 |

13 - 8   _____ – 10 + _____ = _____

20 - 9   _____ – 10 + _____ = _____

30 - 8   _____ – 10 + _____ = _____

30 - 9   _____ – 10 + _____ = _____

How's Your Pitch?

Solve the subtraction problems. Write each answer.

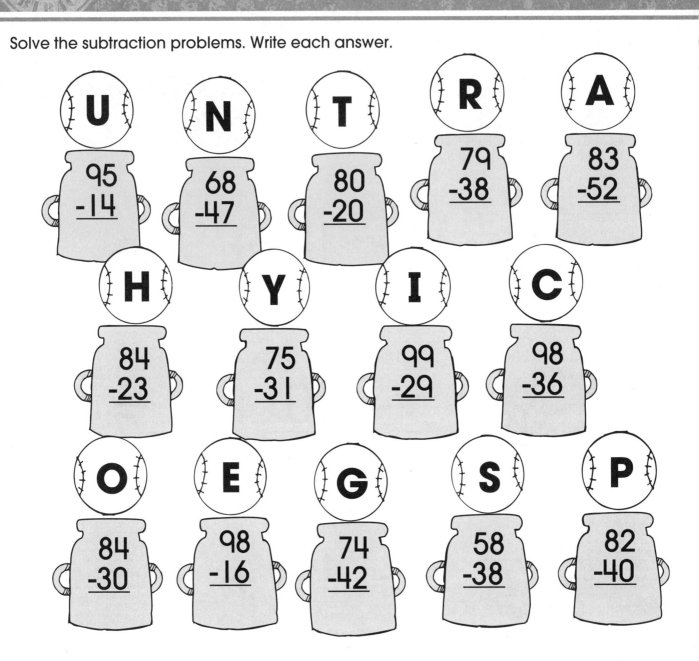

U
95
-14

N
68
-47

T
80
-20

R
79
-38

A
83
-52

H
84
-23

Y
75
-31

I
99
-29

C
98
-36

O
84
-30

E
98
-16

G
74
-42

S
58
-38

P
82
-40

Use the answers and the letters on the baseballs to solve the code.

___ ___ ___ ___   ___ ___ ___ ___ ___   ___ ___
44 54 81 41   42 70 60 62 61   70 20

___ ___ ___ ___ ___   ___ ___   ___ ___ ___ ___ ___ ___ !
41 70 32 61 60   54 21   60 31 41 32 82 60

Prehistoric Problems

Solve the subtraction problems. Use the code to color the picture.

Code: 25 — blue   31 — yellow   21 — brown   57 — green   14 — orange   11 — red

Ready to Regroup

Regrouping is using one ten to form ten ones, one 100 to form ten tens, and so on.

Study the examples. Follow the steps to subtract.

Example:

```
   2 8
 - 1 4
```

Step 1:
Regroup.

tens	ones
2	17
~~3~~	~~7~~
− 1	9

Step 2:
Subtract the ones.

tens	ones
2	17
~~3~~	~~7~~
− 1	9
	8

Step 3:
Subtract the tens.

tens	ones
2	17
~~3~~	~~7~~
− 1	9
1	8

```
   2 8          4 6          1 2
 - 1 9        - 1 8        -   8
```

```
   3 0          5 2          4 7
 - 1 2        - 2 5        - 3 5
```

Two-Digit Subtraction

Solve the problems.

63 − 48	83 − 45	74 − 29	94 − 48	62 − 25
45 − 27	33 − 24	24 − 8	86 − 37	72 − 48
36 − 17	26 − 18	43 − 19	63 − 48	93 − 18
82 − 26	73 − 28	95 − 69	57 − 38	41 − 25

What's the Difference?

Solve each problem.

tens	ones
5	4
- 1	7

tens	ones
3	3
- 1	5

tens	ones
6	1
- 3	3

tens	ones
2	7
- 1	6

tens	ones
4	2
- 2	4

tens	ones
5	2
- 2	6

tens	ones
9	4
- 4	8

tens	ones
7	7
- 3	4

tens	ones
6	5
- 2	6

Subtraction Challenge

Solve each problem.

Anton sees 55 cars.

37 cars drive away. — ⬜⬜

How many cars are left? ⬜⬜

Hayley sees 81 leaves.

24 blow away. — ⬜⬜

How many leaves are left? ⬜⬜

Jai has 75 dollars.

He spends 26 dollars. — ⬜⬜

How many dollars are left? ⬜⬜

Abbie sees 31 boats.

12 boats leave. — ⬜⬜

How many boats are left? ⬜⬜

Undersea Adventure

Solve the subtraction problems below.

tens	ones
4	7
- 2	8

tens	ones
6	4
- 3	4

tens	ones
5	3
- 3	9

```
  73        56
- 66      - 27

  35        83
- 14      - 47

  43        75
- 39      - 53

  67        26
- 58      -  7
```

Brainy Book of Addition and Subtraction

Subtract and Solve

Solve each problem.

Neil and Ty play 24 games.

Neil wins 17 games.

How many did Ty win?

Yelena sees 72 boxes.

64 boxes get moved.

How many boxes are left?

Krystal has 48 pens.

She loses 19.

How many pens are left?

Xander sees 37 ants.

18 ants go in the anthill.

How many ants are left?

Square Subtraction

Use the hundred board to solve each problem. Circle the first number in the problem on the board. Then, draw a path on the board as you count back to subtract the second number. Draw a triangle around the answer. Write the answer to complete the number sentence.

22 – 11 = _____   67 – 14 = _____   36 – 9 = _____

88 – 12 = _____   94 – 5 = _____   51 – 12 = _____

1	2	3	4	5	6	7	8	9	10
11	12	13	14	15	16	17	18	19	20
21	22	23	24	25	26	27	28	29	30
31	32	33	34	35	36	37	38	39	40
41	42	43	44	45	46	47	48	49	50
51	52	53	54	55	56	57	58	59	60
61	62	63	64	65	66	67	68	69	70
71	72	73	74	75	76	77	78	79	80
81	82	83	84	85	86	87	88	89	90
91	92	93	94	95	96	97	98	99	100

Square Subtraction

Use the hundred board to solve each problem. Circle the first number in the problem on the board. Then, draw a path on the board as you count back to subtract the second number. Draw a triangle around the answer. Write the answer to complete the number sentence.

31 – 10 = _____

57 – 13 = _____

19 – 8 = _____

77 – 12 = _____

99 – 6 = _____

88 – 10 = _____

1	2	3	4	5	6	7	8	9	10
11	12	13	14	15	16	17	18	19	20
21	22	23	24	25	26	27	28	29	30
31	32	33	34	35	36	37	38	39	40
41	42	43	44	45	46	47	48	49	50
51	52	53	54	55	56	57	58	59	60
61	62	63	64	65	66	67	68	69	70
71	72	73	74	75	76	77	78	79	80
81	82	83	84	85	86	87	88	89	90
91	92	93	94	95	96	97	98	99	100

Problem Solving

Write a number sentence to solve each problem.

Example:

Dad cooks 23 potatoes.
He used 19 potatoes in the potato salad.
How many potatoes are left?

23 – 19 = 4

Susan draws 32 butterflies.
She colors 15 of them brown.
How many butterflies does she have left to color?

_____

A book has 66 pages.
Pedro reads 39 pages.
How many pages are left to read?

_____

Jerry picks up 34 sea shells.
He puts 15 of them in a box.
How many does he have left?

_____

Name _____

Subtraction Challenge

Solve each problem.

There are 58 trucks.

49 trucks drive away. —

How many trucks are left?

Abe can run 36 miles.

He runs 17 miles. —

How many miles are left?

Uma lives 38 miles away.

She has gone 38 miles. —

How many miles are left?

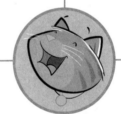

Zane has 62 balloons.

39 balloons fly away. —

How many balloons are left?

A Day at the Beach

Subtract to find the difference. Regroup as needed. Color the spaces with differences of:

10 — 19: red   50 — 59: brown   30 — 39: green

40 — 49: yellow   20 — 29: blue   60 — 69: orange

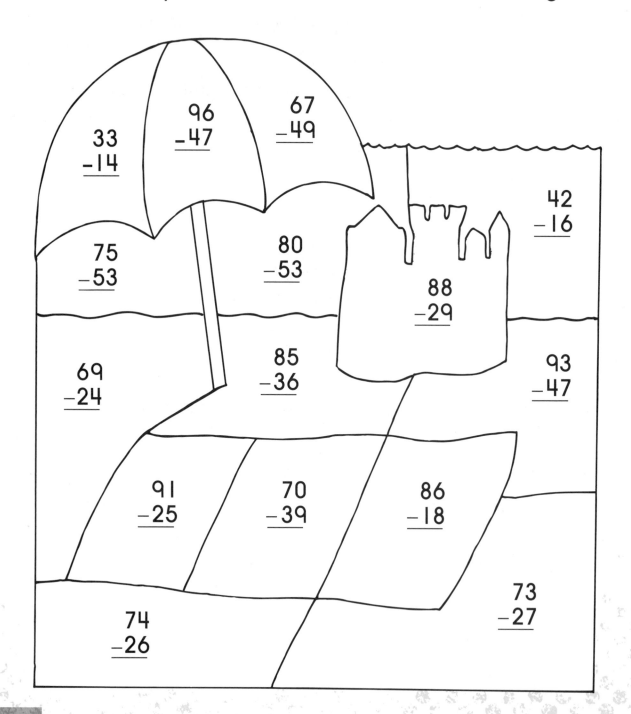

$$\begin{array}{r}96\\-47\\\hline\end{array}$$

$$\begin{array}{r}67\\-49\\\hline\end{array}$$

$$\begin{array}{r}33\\-14\\\hline\end{array}$$

$$\begin{array}{r}42\\-16\\\hline\end{array}$$

$$\begin{array}{r}75\\-53\\\hline\end{array}$$

$$\begin{array}{r}80\\-53\\\hline\end{array}$$

$$\begin{array}{r}88\\-29\\\hline\end{array}$$

$$\begin{array}{r}69\\-24\\\hline\end{array}$$

$$\begin{array}{r}85\\-36\\\hline\end{array}$$

$$\begin{array}{r}93\\-47\\\hline\end{array}$$

$$\begin{array}{r}91\\-25\\\hline\end{array}$$

$$\begin{array}{r}70\\-39\\\hline\end{array}$$

$$\begin{array}{r}86\\-18\\\hline\end{array}$$

$$\begin{array}{r}73\\-27\\\hline\end{array}$$

$$\begin{array}{r}74\\-26\\\hline\end{array}$$

Add or Subtract?

Write + or − in the circles. Then, solve the problems.

1. The pet store has 3 large dogs and 5 small dogs. How many dogs are there in all?

3 ◯ 5 = _____

2. The pet store had 9 parrots and then sold 4 of them. How many parrots does the pet store have left?

9 ◯ 4 = _____

4. The pet store gave Linda's class 2 adult gerbils and 9 young ones. How many gerbils did Linda's class get in all?

2 ◯ 9 = _____

3. At the pet store, 3 of the 8 kittens were sold. How many kittens are left in the pet store?

8 ◯ 3 = _____

5. The monkey at the pet store has 5 rubber toys and 4 wooden toys. How many toys does the monkey have in all?

5 ◯ 4 = _____

Wings and Water

Draw a line under the question that matches the picture. Then, solve the problems.

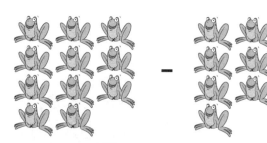

How many s are there in all?
How many s are left?

$$11 - 7 = \rule{2cm}{0.4pt}$$

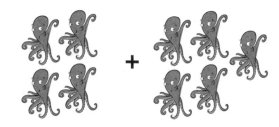

How many s are there in all?
How many s are left?

$$4 + 5 = \rule{2cm}{0.4pt}$$

How many s are there in all?
How many s are left?

$$8 - 3 = \rule{2cm}{0.4pt}$$

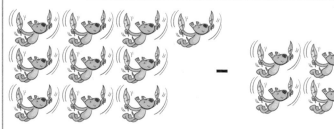

How many s are there in all?
How many s are left?

$$10 - 4 = \rule{2cm}{0.4pt}$$

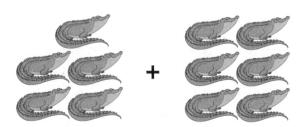

How many s are there in all?
How many s are left?

$$5 + 6 = \rule{2cm}{0.4pt}$$

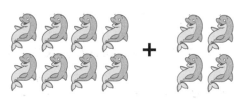

How many s are there in all?
How many s are left?

$$8 + 4 = \rule{2cm}{0.4pt}$$

Color the Fruit

Solve the subtraction sentences below. Use the code to color the fruit.

3 — yellow	5 — orange	7 — yellow	9 — red
4 — red	6 — purple	8 — green	10 — brown

$$\begin{array}{r} 9 \\ -\ 4 \\ \hline \end{array}$$

$$\begin{array}{r} 3 \\ +\ 7 \\ \hline \end{array}$$

$$\begin{array}{r} 6 \\ -\ 3 \\ \hline \end{array}$$

$$\begin{array}{r} 1 \\ +\ 3 \\ \hline \end{array}$$

$$\begin{array}{r} 9 \\ -\ 2 \\ \hline \end{array}$$

$$\begin{array}{r} 7 \\ +\ 2 \\ \hline \end{array}$$

$$\begin{array}{r} 9 \\ -\ 1 \\ \hline \end{array}$$

$$\begin{array}{r} 6 \\ +\ 3 \\ \hline \end{array}$$

$$\begin{array}{r} 8 \\ -\ 2 \\ \hline \end{array}$$

Move That Animal!

Write the number that each animal is hiding.

$2 + $  $ = 5$

 $ = $ _ _ _ _ _ _ _

$7 - $ $ = 4$

$ = $ _ _ _ _ _ _ _

$ - 5 = 2$

$ = $ _ _ _ _ _ _ _

Hidden Numbers

Write the number that each animal is hiding.

$$\text{🦁} + 3 = 6$$

$$\text{🦁} = \underline{}$$

$$1 + \text{🐻} = 3$$

$$\text{🐻} = \underline{}$$

$$9 - \text{🦍} = 2$$

$$\text{🦍} = \underline{}$$

Monkey Business

Solve the addition and subtraction problems below.

10 − 6	7 + 3	4 − 2	6 − 2

6 + 4	5 + 4	7 − 1	6 − 3

4 + 3	1 + 9	2 − 1	8 − 6	2 + 1	10 − 3	9 − 4

13 − 5	2 + 8	6 − 3	5 + 5	5 − 3	8 + 2	5 − 4

10 − 8	5 − 1	5 + 2	9 + 2	2 + 6	3 + 7	8 + 1

Name _____

Chugging Along

Solve the addition and subtraction problems below.

$$7 + 2 \qquad 9 - 3 \qquad 2 + 5 \qquad 10 - 7 \qquad 7 - 3 \qquad 4 + 3 \qquad 6 + 3$$

$$8 - 3 \qquad 7 - 6 \qquad 9 - 8 \qquad 10 - 2 \qquad 2 + 5 \qquad 5 + 3 \qquad 3 + 3$$

$$9 - 6 \qquad 6 - 3 \qquad 4 + 5 \qquad 8 - 5 \qquad 6 - 2 \qquad 10 - 9 \qquad 8 - 2$$

$$7 + 1 \qquad 6 + 2 \qquad 3 - 1 \qquad 4 + 2 \qquad 9 - 7 \qquad 4 - 2 \qquad 5 + 2$$

Add or Subtract?

Solve the number problem under each picture. Write + or – to show if you should add or subtract.

How many 's in all?

4 _____ 5 = _____

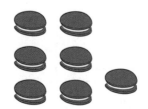 

How many 's in all?

7 _____ 5 = _____

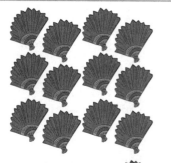  

How many 's are left?

12 _____ 3 = _____

How many 's are left?

15 _____ 8 = _____

How many 's in all?

5 _____ 8 = _____

How many 's are left?

11 _____ 4 = _____

Plus or Minus?

Solve the number problem under each picture. Write + or – to show if you should add or subtract.

How many 's in all?

7   5 = _____

How many 's in all?

8   3 = _____

How many 's are left?

9   4 = _____

How many 's are left?

14   1 = _____

How many 's in all?

15   6 = _____

How many s are left?

9   5 = _____

Blastoff Facts

Write the four facts for each fact family.

6, 9, 15

4, 8, 12

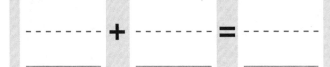

MORE Blastoff Facts

Write the four facts for each fact family.

6, 7, 13

_____ + _____ = _____

_____ + _____ = _____

_____ - _____ = _____

8, 9, 17

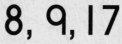

_____ + _____ = _____

_____ + _____ = _____

_____ - _____ = _____

_____ - _____ = _____

Crazy Quilt

Solve the problems. From your answers, use the code to color the quilt.

6 = blue   7 = yellow   8 = green   9 = red   10 = orange

Brainy Book of Addition and Subtraction

Seeing Spots

Each domino represents a fact family. Write the related facts for each fact family.

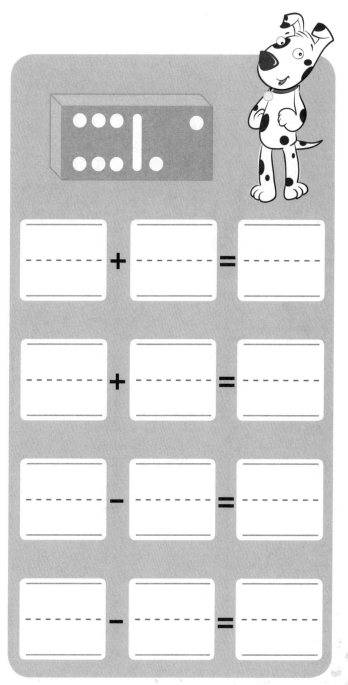

Dots and Spots

Each domino represents a fact family. Write the related facts for each fact family.

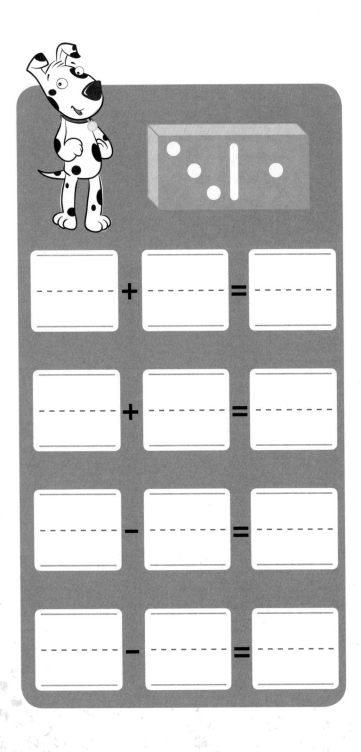

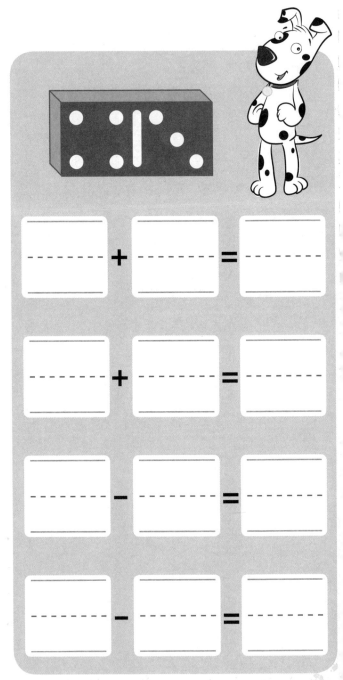

Puppy Problems

Look at the pictures. Write + or – in the circles. Write the answers to the number sentences.

5 ◯ 6 = _____

11 ◯ 4 = _____

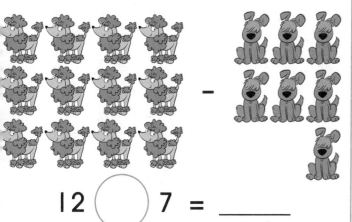

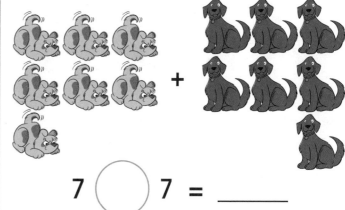

12 ◯ 7 = _____

7 ◯ 7 = _____

5 ◯ 5 = _____

8 ◯ 6 = _____

Add or Subtract?

Write + or – in the magnifying glass to make each problem correct. Circle the four problems that will not work with either sign.

9
5
4

8
7
15

11
4
8

10
4
6

7
9
16

14
6
8

7
7
13

6  7 = 13

13  9 = 4

15  9 = 6

9  2 = 12

10  3 = 6

8  8 = 16

Mystery Signs

Write + or – to make each number sentence true.

$9 \quad \boxed{} \quad 5 = 4$

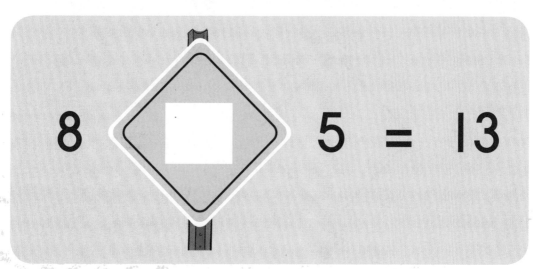

$8 \quad \boxed{} \quad 5 = 13$

Find the Sign

Write + or − to make each number sentence true.

9 ☐ 5 = 14

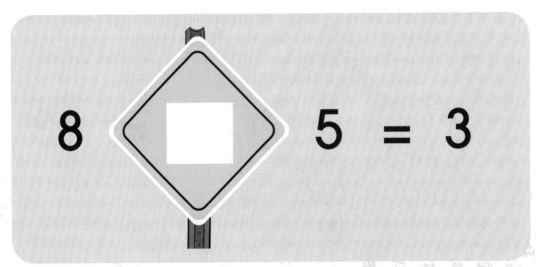

8 ☐ 5 = 3

Name_____

Rabbit Rumpus

Add or subtract to solve each problem. Circle the answers that are less than 10.

Example:

$$\begin{array}{r} 3 \\ + \ 1 \\ \hline \textcircled{4} \end{array} \qquad \begin{array}{r} 3 \\ - \ 1 \\ \hline \textcircled{2} \end{array}$$

$$\begin{array}{r} 9 \\ + \ 3 \\ \hline \end{array} \qquad \begin{array}{r} 6 \\ - \ 2 \\ \hline \end{array} \qquad \begin{array}{r} 12 \\ - \ 1 \\ \hline \end{array} \qquad \begin{array}{r} 18 \\ + \ 1 \\ \hline \end{array} \qquad \begin{array}{r} 15 \\ - \ 6 \\ \hline \end{array}$$

$$\begin{array}{r} 7 \\ + \ 6 \\ \hline \end{array} \qquad \begin{array}{r} 16 \\ - \ 9 \\ \hline \end{array} \qquad \begin{array}{r} 10 \\ - \ 3 \\ \hline \end{array} \qquad \begin{array}{r} 14 \\ + \ 5 \\ \hline \end{array} \qquad \begin{array}{r} 16 \\ - \ 8 \\ \hline \end{array}$$

$$\begin{array}{r} 8 \\ + \ 7 \\ \hline \end{array} \qquad \begin{array}{r} 12 \\ + \ 2 \\ \hline \end{array} \qquad \begin{array}{r} 13 \\ - \ 4 \\ \hline \end{array} \qquad \begin{array}{r} 17 \\ + \ 2 \\ \hline \end{array} \qquad \begin{array}{r} 9 \\ + \ 9 \\ \hline \end{array}$$

Flip It!

Solve each addition problem. Use the addition facts to help you solve each subtraction problem.

18 - 9 = _____

14 - 6 = _____

17 - 8 = _____

15 - 7 = _____

9 + _____ = 18

6 + _____ = 14

8 + _____ = 17

7 + _____ = 15

Switch It Up!

Solve each addition problem. Use the addition facts to help you solve each subtraction problem.

18 - 8 = _____   8 + _____ = 18

14 - 5 = _____   5 + _____ = 14

17 - 6 = _____   6 + _____ = 17

15 - 4 = _____   4 + _____ = 15

Dip into Dominoes

Count the dots on each side of each domino. Then, write the related facts for each domino.

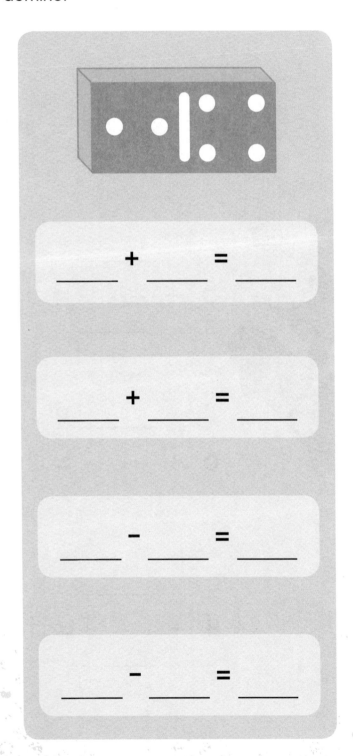

_____ + _____ = _____

_____ + _____ = _____

_____ - _____ = _____

_____ - _____ = _____

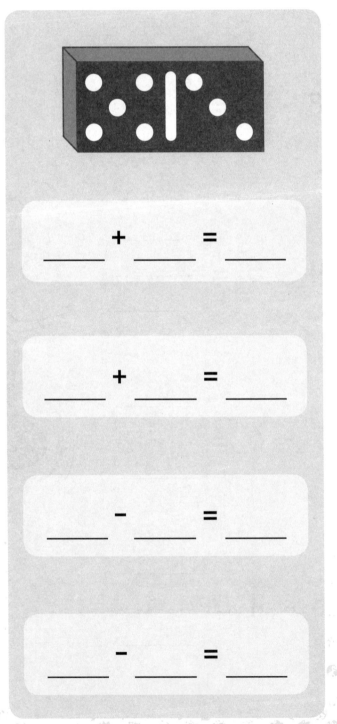

_____ + _____ = _____

_____ + _____ = _____

_____ - _____ = _____

_____ - _____ = _____

Elevator Operator

Look at the first and last numbers in each number sentence. Did the first number go up or down to become the last number? Circle the correct elevator button beside the number sentence. Write + or – in the blank to make the sentence true.

Up 15 ____ 5 = 20

Down

30 ____ 19 = 11 **Up**

Down

Up 11 ____ 14 = 25

Down

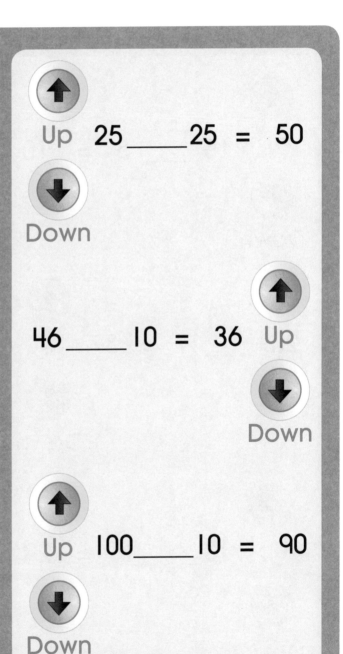

Up 25 ____ 25 = 50

Down

46 ____ 10 = 36 **Up**

Down

Up 100 ____ 10 = 90

Down

Up or Down?

Look at the first and last numbers in each number sentence. Did the first number go up or down to become the last number? Circle the correct elevator button beside the number sentence. Write + or – in the blank to make the sentence true.

Up 15 _____ 5 = 10

Down

Up 33 _____ 33 = 66

Down

20 _____ 17 = 37
 Up

Down

57 _____ 10 = 47
 Up
Down

Up 13 _____ 16 = 29

Down

Up 100 _____ 20 = 80

Down

True or False?

Decide if each statement is true or false. Circle **T** for true or **F** for false.

If 3 + 4 = 7, then 4 + 3 = 7.　　　　　　T　　F

If 20 + 0 = 20, then 0 + 20 = 20.　　　　T　　F

If 3 + 4 + 4 + 2 = 13, then 13 = 2 + 4 + 4 + 3.　　T　　F

If 12 − 0 = 12, then 0 − 12 = 12.　　　　T　　F

If 23 + 50 = 73, then 73 = 50 + 23.　　　T　　F

If 18 − 9 = 9, then 9 = 9 − 18.　　　　　T　　F

True or False?

Decide if each statement is true or false. Circle **T** for true or **F** for false.

If 3 + 5 = 8, then 5 + 3 = 8.　　　　　　T　　F

If 30 + 0 = 30, then 0 + 30 = 30.　　　　T　　F

If 2 + 3 + 3 + 5 = 13, then 13 = 5 + 3 + 3 + 2.　　T　　F

If 13 – 0 = 13, then 0 – 13 = 13.　　　　T　　F

If 33 + 60 = 93, then 93 = 60 + 33.　　　T　　F

If 17 – 8 = 9, then 9 = 8 – 17.　　　　　T　　F

Symbol Substitute

Figure out the missing number behind each picture. Then, write the number.

40 + 🏵 = 50

🏵 = _____

🍭 − 70 = 50

🍭 = _____

10 + ⚽ = 30

⚽ = _____

80 − ☁ = 20

☁ = _____

Find the Number

Figure out the missing number behind each picture. Then, write the number.

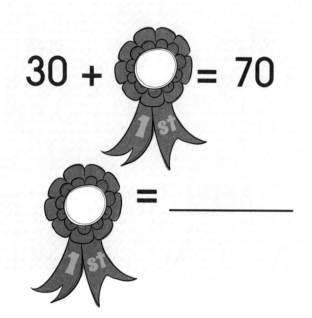

30 + 🎗 = 70

🎗 = _____

🍭 − 60 = 30

🍭 = _____

20 + ⚽ = 40

⚽ = _____

90 − ☁ = 60

☁ = _____

Name _____

Go "Fore" It!

Add or subtract using regrouping.

$$\begin{array}{r} 40 \\ -16 \\ \hline \end{array}$$

$$\begin{array}{r} 35 \\ +27 \\ \hline \end{array}$$

$$\begin{array}{r} 56 \\ -27 \\ \hline \end{array}$$

$$\begin{array}{r} 42 \\ -14 \\ \hline \end{array}$$

$$\begin{array}{r} 44 \\ +28 \\ \hline \end{array}$$

$$\begin{array}{r} 93 \\ -39 \\ \hline \end{array}$$

$$\begin{array}{r} 56 \\ -17 \\ \hline \end{array}$$

$$\begin{array}{r} 97 \\ -48 \\ \hline \end{array}$$

$$\begin{array}{r} 73 \\ -24 \\ \hline \end{array}$$

$$\begin{array}{r} 33 \\ +18 \\ \hline \end{array}$$

$$\begin{array}{r} 68 \\ -49 \\ \hline \end{array}$$

$$\begin{array}{r} 77 \\ -68 \\ \hline \end{array}$$

$$\begin{array}{r} 49 \\ -32 \\ \hline \end{array}$$

$$\begin{array}{r} 27 \\ -19 \\ \hline \end{array}$$

Brainy Book of Addition and Subtraction

Monster Math

Add or subtract using regrouping.

```
  84        33        36
- 56      - 15      - 19
```

```
  41                  65
- 17                - 28
```

```
  52                  48
- 28                - 30
```

```
  84                  33
- 27                + 18
```

```
  57        72        64        25
- 39      - 19      + 17      + 35
```

Brainy Book of Addition and Subtraction

Adding Hundreds

Solve the problems.

3 hundreds	300	6 hundreds	600
+1 hundreds	+100	+2 hundreds	+200
4 hundreds	**400**	hundreds	

200	100	600	400
+ 200	+ 700	+ 300	+ 500

300	800	400	700
+ 400	+ 100	+ 400	+ 200

500	100	500	300
+ 100	+ 600	+ 200	+ 200

300	400	300	200
+ 300	+ 200	+ 500	+ 100

Building Numbers

Look at the examples. Follow the steps to add.

Example:

hundreds	tens	ones		hundreds	tens	ones		hundreds	tens	ones
	1				1				1	
3	4	**8**		3	4	8		**3**	4	8
+ 4	4	**4**		+ 4	4	4		+ **4**	4	4
		2			**9**	2		**7**	**9**	2

```
  2 7 1        3 4 5        6 0 9        5 3 7
+ 4 1 9      + 4 3 9      + 2 4 4      + 1 0 9
```

```
  4 1 8        4 7 1        3 3 4
+ 3 2 3      + 3 1 9      + 5 2 8
```

```
  6 5 9        7 3 6        4 2 6
+ 1 2 7      + 1 4 5      + 1 6 5
```

Chalk It Up!

Solve the problems. Regroup when needed.

```
  3 4 8          1 7 2
+ 2 1 4        + 4 1 8
```

```
  6 2 3          3 6 9
+ 2 6 8        + 5 3 3
```

```
  7 3 3          4 1 1          4 2 3
+ 2 2 9        + 2 9 9        + 1 6 9
```

```
  6 2 4          2 7 2          3 9 3
+ 3 6 8        + 4 6 9        + 4 1 8
```

Problem Solving

Solve each problem.

Example:

Ria packed 300 boxes.
Melvin packed 200 boxes.
How many boxes did Ria and Melvin pack?

$$\begin{array}{r} 200 \\ +300 \\ \hline 500 \end{array}$$

Santo typed 500 letters.
Hale typed 400 letters.
How many letters did they type?

Paula used 100 paper clips.
Milton used 600 paper clips.
How many paper clips did they use?

The grocery store sold 400 red apples.
The grocery store also sold 100 yellow apples.
How many apples did the grocery store sell in all?

Subtracting Hundreds

Solve the problems.

9 hundreds	900	3 hundreds	300
−7 hundreds	−700	−1 hundreds	−100
2 hundreds	**200**	hundreds	

```
  700        500        900        800
- 300      - 400      - 400      - 500
```

```
  600        900        500        400
- 100      - 200      - 100      - 200
```

```
  600        300        500        800
- 500      - 200      - 100      - 200
```

Scoops of Fun

Look at the example. Follow the steps to subtract.

Example:
Step 1: Regroup the ones if needed.
Step 2: Subtract the ones.
Step 3: Subtract the tens.
Step 4: Subtract the hundreds.

hundreds	tens	ones
	5	12
4	~~6~~	~~2~~
2	5	3
2	0	9

```
  4 2 3        5 6 2        4 7 8        6 5 1
- 1 1 4      - 3 4 9      - 2 3 9      - 3 3 3
```

Draw a line to the correct answer. Color the ice-cream cones.

```
  3 4 7        1 4 4        9 6 3        7 6 2        2 8 7
- 2 1 8      - 1 3 5      - 7 4 8      - 5 5 3      - 1 7 9
```

 2 1 5

 2 0 9

 1 2 9

 1 0 8

 9

Bowl 'Em Over

Subtract. Circle the 7s that appear in the 10s place.

Example:

$$\begin{array}{r} 4\ 9\ 2 \\ -\ 2\ 2\ 1 \\ \hline 2\ 7\ 1 \end{array}$$

$$\begin{array}{r} 358 \\ -238 \\ \hline \end{array}$$

$$\begin{array}{r} 184 \\ -129 \\ \hline \end{array}$$

$$\begin{array}{r} 128 \\ -109 \\ \hline \end{array}$$

$$\begin{array}{r} 744 \\ -674 \\ \hline \end{array}$$

$$\begin{array}{r} 765 \\ -326 \\ \hline \end{array}$$

$$\begin{array}{r} 584 \\ -435 \\ \hline \end{array}$$

$$\begin{array}{r} 693 \\ -314 \\ \hline \end{array}$$

$$\begin{array}{r} 835 \\ -217 \\ \hline \end{array}$$

$$\begin{array}{r} 248 \\ -199 \\ \hline \end{array}$$

$$\begin{array}{r} 635 \\ -428 \\ \hline \end{array}$$

$$\begin{array}{r} 921 \\ -362 \\ \hline \end{array}$$

$$\begin{array}{r} 432 \\ -314 \\ \hline \end{array}$$

Add and Subtract

Solve each problem.

973 people live in Littleville.

139 people move away.

$-$ [ ][ ][ ]

[ ][ ][ ]

How many people are left?

[ ][ ][ ]

Mia has 652 trading cards.

She buys 319 more.

$+$ [ ][ ][ ]

[ ][ ][ ]

How many trading cards does Mia have in all?

[ ][ ][ ]

The Lopez family has driven 289 miles.

The beach is still 234 miles away.

$+$ [ ][ ][ ]

[ ][ ][ ]

How many miles in all will the family drive to reach the beach?

[ ][ ][ ]

---

736 students attend Tomas's school.

249 of the students play on sports teams.

$-$ [ ][ ][ ]

[ ][ ][ ]

How many students do not play on sports teams?

[ ][ ][ ]

Answer Key

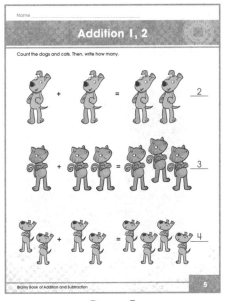

Page 5

Page 6

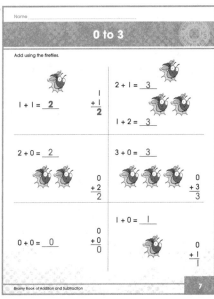

Page 7

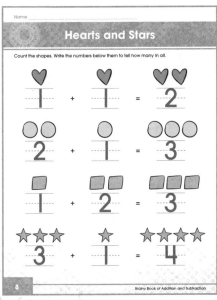

Page 8

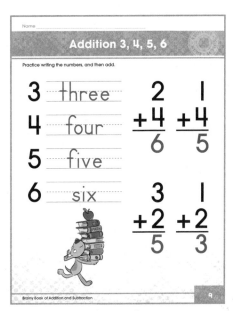

Page 9

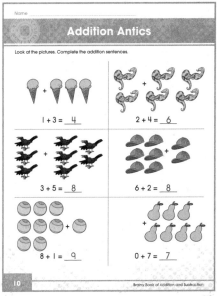

Page 10

Answer Key

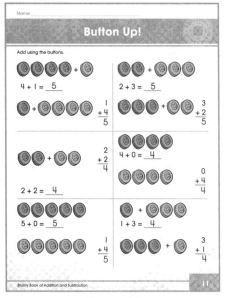

Page 11

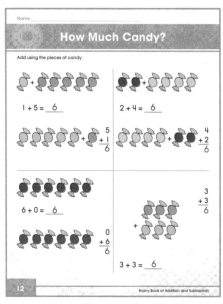

Page 12

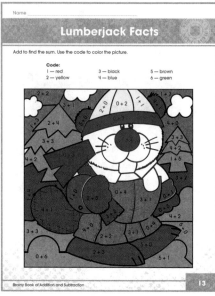

Page 13

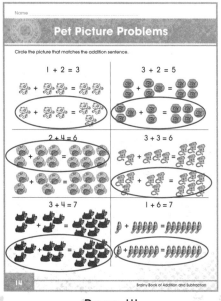

Page 14

Page 15

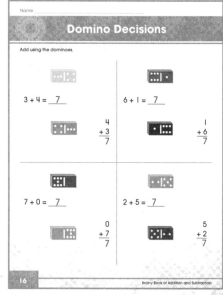

Page 16

Answer Key

ADDITION SUBTRACTION

Sum Flower

Add to find each sum.

If the sum is **6**, color the area **blue**.

If the sum is **7**, color the area **yellow**.

Page 17

Domino Drill

Add using the dominoes.

$5 + 3 = \underline{8}$

$7 + 1 = \underline{8}$

$\begin{array}{r} 3 \\ + 5 \\ \hline 8 \end{array}$

$\begin{array}{r} 1 \\ + 7 \\ \hline 8 \end{array}$

$2 + 6 = \underline{8}$

$\begin{array}{r} 6 \\ + 2 \\ \hline 8 \end{array}$

$\begin{array}{r} 4 \\ + 4 \\ \hline 8 \end{array}$

$4 + 4 = \underline{8}$

Page 18

Fresh Fruit Facts

Draw pictures to show what happens in each story. Solve the problem.

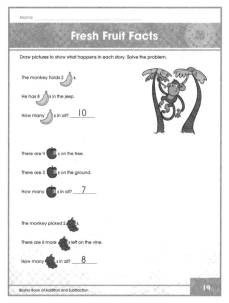

The monkey holds 2 🍌 s.

He has 8 🍌 s in the jeep.

How many 🍌 s in all? __10__

There are 4 🍎 s on the tree.

There are 3 🍎 s on the ground.

How many 🍎 s in all? __7__

The monkey picked 2 🍇 s.

There are 6 more 🍇 s left on the vine.

How many 🍇 s in all? __8__

Page 19

Bear Necessities

How many more are needed? Draw the missing pictures. Complete the addition sentences.

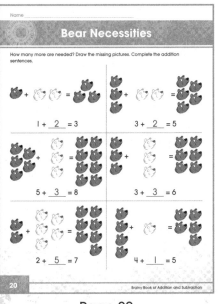

$1 + \underline{2} = 3$

$3 + \underline{2} = 5$

$5 + \underline{3} = 8$

$3 + \underline{3} = 6$

$2 + \underline{5} = 7$

$4 + \underline{1} = 5$

Page 20

Domino Domination

Add using the dominoes.

$2 + 7 = \underline{9}$

$5 + 4 = \underline{9}$

$\begin{array}{r} 7 \\ + 2 \\ \hline 9 \end{array}$

$\begin{array}{r} 4 \\ + 5 \\ \hline 9 \end{array}$

$1 + 8 = \underline{9}$

$3 + 6 = \underline{9}$

$\begin{array}{r} 8 \\ + 1 \\ \hline 9 \end{array}$

$\begin{array}{r} 6 \\ + 3 \\ \hline 9 \end{array}$

$\begin{array}{r} 0 \\ + 9 \\ \hline 9 \end{array}$

$\begin{array}{r} 9 \\ + 0 \\ \hline 9 \end{array}$

$0 + 9 = \underline{9}$

$9 + 0 = \underline{9}$

Page 21

Robot Invasion

Complete the addition sentences.

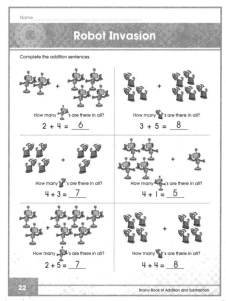

How many 🤖's are there in all?
$2 + 4 = \underline{6}$

How many 🤖's are there in all?
$3 + 5 = \underline{8}$

How many 🤖's are there in all?
$4 + 3 = \underline{7}$

How many 🤖's are there in all?
$4 + 1 = \underline{5}$

How many 🤖's are there in all?
$2 + 5 = \underline{7}$

How many 🤖's are there in all?
$4 + 4 = \underline{8}$

Page 22

Answer Key

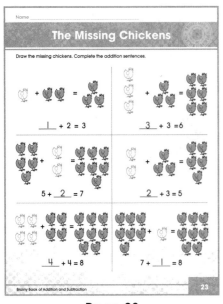

Page 23

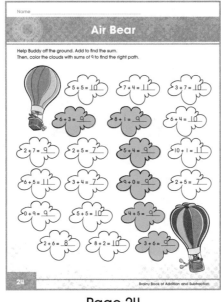

Page 24

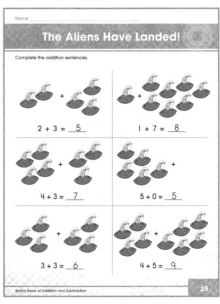

Page 25

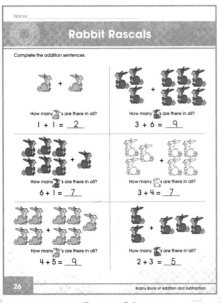

Page 26

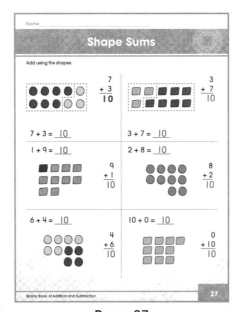

Page 27

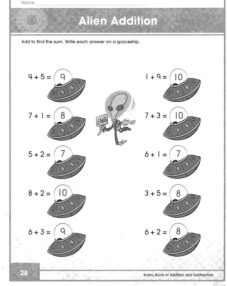

Page 28

Answer Key

Brainy Book of Addition and Subtraction

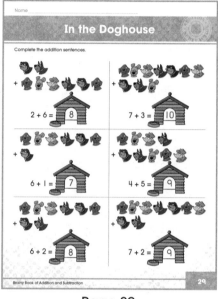

In the Doghouse

Complete the addition sentences.

2 + 6 = **8**

7 + 3 = **10**

6 + 1 = **7**

4 + 5 = **9**

6 + 2 = **8**

7 + 2 = **9**

Page 29

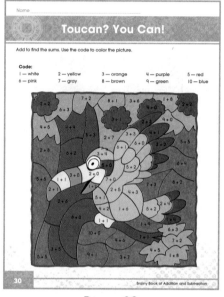

Toucan? You Can!

Add to find the sums. Use the code to color the picture.

Code:
1 — white   2 — yellow   3 — orange   4 — purple   5 — red
6 — pink   7 — gray   8 — brown   9 — green   10 — blue

Page 30

Ready to Roll!

Roll a die. Write the number from the die in the top box. Add to find the sum.
Roll again to make each sentence different.

5
+ 1
6

Answers will vary.

+ 2   + 2   + 3   + 2   + 1

+ 3   + 2   + 3   + 3   + 2

Page 31

Counting Up

Count up to get the sum. Write the missing number in each blank.

3 + **3** = 6
4 + **1** = 5
7 + **2** = 9
2 + **2** = 4
3 + **5** = 8
5 + **0** = 5
8 + **2** = 10
7 + **1** = 8
6 + **3** = 9

8 + **1** = 9
4 + **2** = 6
6 + **0** = 6
5 + **2** = 7
4 + **3** = 7
9 + **1** = 10
5 + **3** = 8
7 + **3** = 10
6 + **2** = 8

Page 32

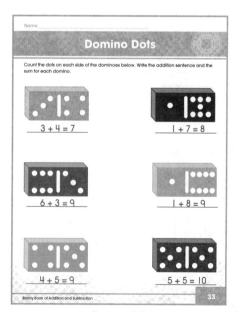

Domino Dots

Count the dots on each side of the dominoes below. Write the addition sentence and the sum for each domino.

3 + 4 = 7

1 + 7 = 8

6 + 3 = 9

1 + 8 = 9

4 + 5 = 9

5 + 5 = 10

Page 33

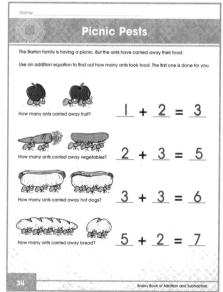

Picnic Pests

The Barton family is having a picnic. But the ants have carried away their food.

Use an addition equation to find out how many ants took food. The first one is done for you.

How many ants carried away fruit?   **1** + **2** = **3**

How many ants carried away vegetables?   **2** + **3** = **5**

How many ants carried away hot dogs?   **3** + **3** = **6**

How many ants carried away bread?   **5** + **2** = **7**

Page 34

Answer Key

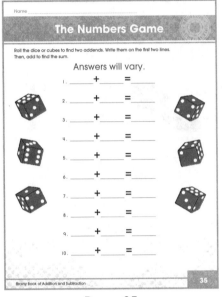

The Numbers Game

Roll the dice or cubes to find two addends. Write them on the first two lines. Then, add to find the sum.

Answers will vary.

1. _____ + _____ = _____
2. _____ + _____ = _____
3. _____ + _____ = _____
4. _____ + _____ = _____
5. _____ + _____ = _____
6. _____ + _____ = _____
7. _____ + _____ = _____
8. _____ + _____ = _____
9. _____ + _____ = _____
10. _____ + _____ = _____

Page 35

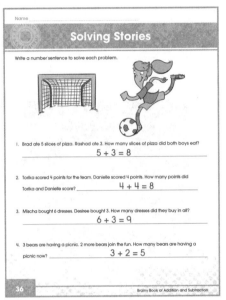

Solving Stories

Write a number sentence to solve each problem.

1. Brad ate 5 slices of pizza. Rashad ate 3. How many slices of pizza did both boys eat?
$5 + 3 = 8$

2. Torika scored 4 points for the team. Danielle scored 4 points. How many points did Torika and Danielle score?
$4 + 4 = 8$

3. Mischa bought 6 dresses. Desiree bought 3. How many dresses did they buy in all?
$6 + 3 = 9$

4. 3 bears are having a picnic. 2 more bears join the fun. How many bears are having a picnic now?
$3 + 2 = 5$

Page 36

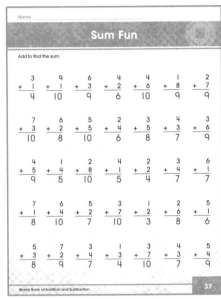

Sum Fun

Add to find the sum.

3 +1 = 4	9 +1 = 10	6 +3 = 9	4 +2 = 6	4 +6 = 10	1 +8 = 9	2 +7 = 9
7 +3 = 10	6 +2 = 8	5 +5 = 10	2 +4 = 6	3 +5 = 8	4 +3 = 7	3 +6 = 9
4 +5 = 9	1 +4 = 5	2 +8 = 10	4 +1 = 5	2 +2 = 4	3 +4 = 7	6 +1 = 7
7 +1 = 8	6 +4 = 10	5 +2 = 7	3 +7 = 10	1 +2 = 3	2 +6 = 8	5 +1 = 6
5 +3 = 8	7 +2 = 9	3 +4 = 7	1 +3 = 4	3 +7 = 10	4 +3 = 7	5 +4 = 9

Page 37

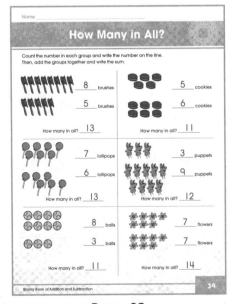

Fill the Grid!

Write the sums where the columns and rows meet. The first one shows you what to do.

+	1	2	3	4	5	6	7	8	9
1	2	3	4	5	6	7	8	9	10
2	3	4	5	6	7	8	9	10	11
3	4	5	6	7	8	9	10	11	12
4	5	6	7	8	9	10	11	12	13
5	6	7	8	9	10	11	12	13	14
6	7	8	9	10	11	12	13	14	15
7	8	9	10	11	12	13	14	15	16
8	9	10	11	12	13	14	15	16	17
9	10	11	12	13	14	15	16	17	18

Page 38

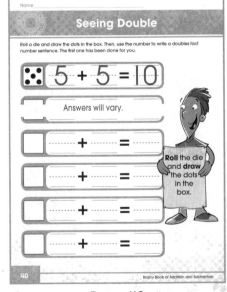

How Many in All?

Count the number in each group and write the number on the line. Then, add the groups together and write the sum.

8 brushes
5 brushes
How many in all? 13

5 cookies
6 cookies
How many in all? 11

7 lollipops
6 lollipops
How many in all? 13

3 puppets
9 puppets
How many in all? 12

8 balls
3 balls
How many in all? 11

7 flowers
7 flowers
How many in all? 14

Page 39

Seeing Double

Roll a die and draw the dots in the box. Then, use the number to write a doubles fact number sentence. The first one has been done for you.

$5 + 5 = 10$

Answers will vary.

_____ + _____ = _____
_____ + _____ = _____
_____ + _____ = _____
_____ + _____ = _____

Roll the die and draw the dots in the box.

Page 40

Answer Key

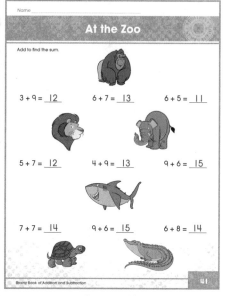

Page 41

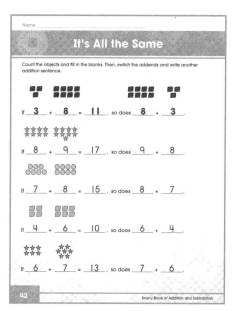

Page 42

Page 43

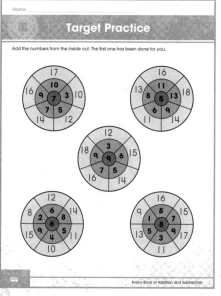

Page 44

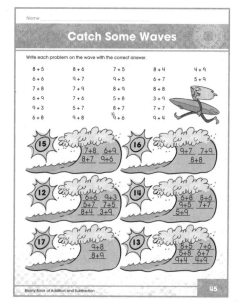

Page 45

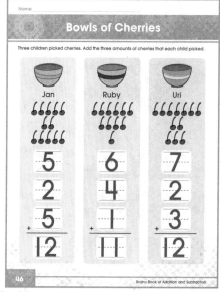

Page 46

Answer Key

ADDITION · SUBTRACTION

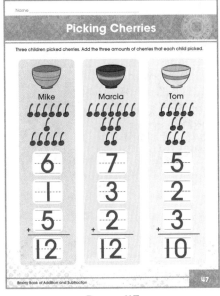

Page 47

Page 48

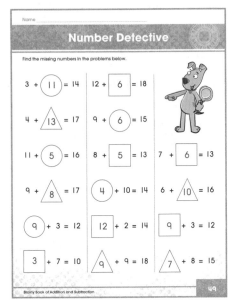

Page 49

Page 50

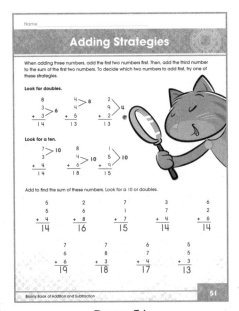

Page 51

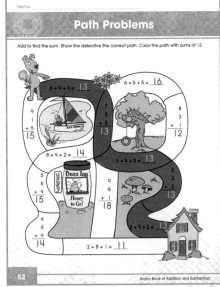

Page 52

Answer Key

Page 53

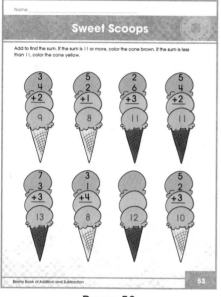

Sweet Scoops

Add to find the sum. If the sum is 11 or more, color the cone brown. If the sum is less than 11, color the cone yellow.

3 4 +2 = 9
5 2 +1 = 8
2 6 +3 = 11
5 4 +2 = 11

7 3 +3 = 13
3 1 +4 = 8
+ = 12
5 2 +3 = 10

Brainy Book of Addition and Subtraction — 53

Page 54

Zero the Hero

Write each missing number to complete the addition facts with zero.

15 + 0 = 15

15 + 0 = 15

0 + 18 = 18

54 — Brainy Book of Addition and Subtraction

Page 55

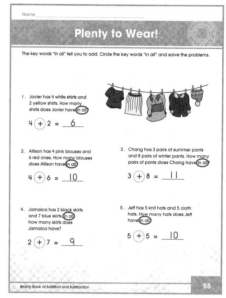

Plenty to Wear!

The key words "in all" tell you to add. Circle the key words "in all" and solve the problems.

1. Javier has 4 white shirts and 2 yellow shirts. How many shirts does Javier have in all?
4 + 2 = 6

2. Allison has 4 pink blouses and 6 red ones. How many blouses does Allison have in all?
4 + 6 = 10

3. Chang has 3 pairs of summer pants and 8 pairs of winter pants. How many pairs of pants does Chang have in all?
3 + 8 = 11

4. Jamaica has 2 black skirts and 7 blue skirts in all how many skirts does Jamaica have?
2 + 7 = 9

5. Jeff has 5 knit hats and 5 cloth hats. How many hats does Jeff have in all?
5 + 5 = 10

Brainy Book of Addition and Subtraction — 55

Page 56

Adventure Island

Count on to solve each problem. The common sum is the spot where the pirate buried his treasure. Mark the spot on the number line with an X.

0 1 2 3 4 5 6 7 8 9 10 11 12 13 14 15 16 17 18 19 20

10 +8 = 18
14 +4 = 18
16 +2 = 18
11 +7 = 18
9 +9 = 18
15 +3 = 18

56 — Brainy Book of Addition and Subtraction

Page 57

"X" Marks the Spot

Count on to solve each problem. The common sum is the spot where the pirate buried his treasure. Mark the spot on the number line with an X.

0 1 2 3 4 5 6 7 8 9 10 11 12 13 14 15 16 17 18 19 20

10 +6 = 16
12 +4 = 16
14 +2 = 16
11 +5 = 16
8 +8 = 16
13 +3 = 16

Brainy Book of Addition and Subtraction — 57

Page 58

Ancient Adding

Roll a pair of dice. Write the number from each die on the lines below. Add to find the sum. Roll again to make each sentence different.

___ + ___ = ___   ___ + ___ = ___

Answers will vary.

___ + ___ = ___   ___ + ___ = ___

___ + ___ = ___   ___ + ___ = ___

___ + ___ = ___   ___ + ___ = ___

___ + ___ = ___   ___ + ___ = ___

___ + ___ = ___   ___ + ___ = ___

58 — Brainy Book of Addition and Subtraction

Answer Key

Camping Solutions

Add the numbers in each sleeping bag. Write the sums. Color in the four largest answers.

5 + 6 = 11   9 + 8 = 17   5 + 1 = 6   9 + 7 = 16

8 + 6 = 14   7 + 7 = 14   9 + 9 = 18   2 + 9 = 11

10 + 10 = 20   9 + 5 = 14   6 + 9 = 15   7 + 6 = 13

Page 59

Zero the Hero Returns!

Write each missing number to complete the addition facts with zero.

11 + 0 = 11

16 + 0 = 16

0 + 20 = 20

Page 60

You "Can" Do It!

Add to find each sum. Connect the dots in order. Use the sums and letters from the box to answer the riddle.

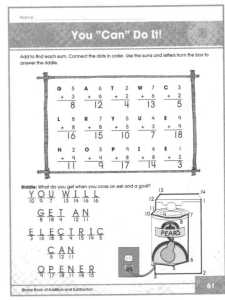

G 5	A 6	T 2	W 7	C 3
+ 3	+ 6	+ 2	+ 6	+ 2
8	12	4	13	5

L 8	R 7	Y 5	U 4	E 9
+ 8	+ 8	+ 5	+ 3	+ 9
16	15	10	7	18

N 2	O 5	P 9	I 6	E 1
+ 9	+ 4	+ 8	+ 8	+ 2
11	9	17	14	3

Riddle: What do you get when you cross an eel and a goat?

Y O U   W I L L
10 9 17 13 16 16

G E T   A N
8 18 4   12 11

E L E C T R I C
3 16 4 5 4 15 14 5

C A N
5 12 11

O P E N E R
9 17 18 11 18 15

Page 61

Racing Riddle

Solve each row from left to right. Write the letters on the lines below to answer the riddle.

E 3	H 2	S 4	Y 7	A 4	O 7
+ 7	+ 1	+ 7	+ 3	+ 8	+ 2
14	12	15	19	17	16

B 9	P 8	T 9	I 5	V 6	R 9
+ 8	+ 4	+ 6	+ 1	+ 3	+ 6
22	18	24	8	11	21

Riddle: What do a race car and a zebra have in common?

B O T H   H A V E
22 16 24 12   12 17 11 14

S T R I P E S
15 24 21 8 18 14 15

Page 62

Add and Laugh

Add to find the sums. Write the letters on the lines.

M	M	A
7 + 3 + 1 = 11	7 + 0 + 2 = 9	6 + 4 + 5 = 15
C	**Y**	**M**
5 + 6 + 3 = 14	2 + 2 + 6 = 10	5 + 3 + 5 = 13
M	**R**	**Y**
8 + 2 + 7 = 17	5 + 4 + 3 = 12	4 + 2 + 1 = 7
U	**M**	**U**
8 + 3 + 5 = 16	6 + 2 + 0 = 8	8 + 1 + 9 = 18

Riddle: What do you call a mummy who eats crackers in bed?

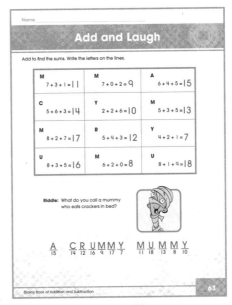

A   C R U M M Y   M U M M Y
15   14 12 16 9 17 7   11 18 13 8 10

Page 63

Race to the Top!

Roll a pair of dice. Color in the box that shows the sum. Which number got to the "top" first?

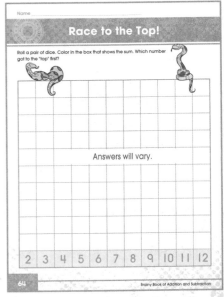

Answers will vary.

| 2 | 3 | 4 | 5 | 6 | 7 | 8 | 9 | 10 | 11 | 12 |

Page 64

Answer Key

Problems in the Park

Name _____

Write a number sentence to solve each problem.

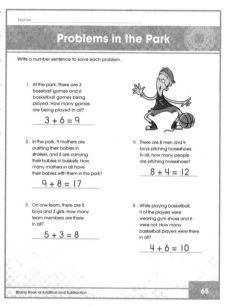

1. At the park, there are 3 baseball games and 6 basketball games being played. How many games are being played in all?

   $3 + 6 = 9$

2. In the park, 9 mothers are pushing their babies in strollers, and 8 are carrying their babies in baskets. How many mothers in all have their babies with them in the park?

   $9 + 8 = 17$

3. On one team, there are 5 boys and 3 girls. How many team members are there in all?

   $5 + 3 = 8$

4. There are 8 men and 4 boys pitching horseshoes. In all, how many people are pitching horseshoes?

   $8 + 4 = 12$

5. While playing basketball, 4 of the players were wearing gym shoes and 6 were not. How many basketball players were there in all?

   $4 + 6 = 10$

Brainy Book of Addition and Subtraction   65

Page 65

Neighborhood Numbers

Name _____

Write a number sentence to solve each problem.

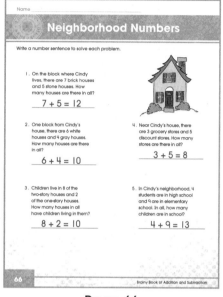

1. On the block where Cindy lives, there are 7 brick houses and 5 stone houses. How many houses are there in all?

   $7 + 5 = 12$

2. One block from Cindy's house, there are 6 white houses and 4 gray houses. How many houses are there in all?

   $6 + 4 = 10$

3. Children live in 8 of the two-story houses and 2 of the one-story houses. How many houses in all have children living in them?

   $8 + 2 = 10$

4. Near Cindy's house, there are 3 grocery stores and 5 discount stores. How many stores are there in all?

   $3 + 5 = 8$

5. In Cindy's neighborhood, 4 students are in high school and 9 are in elementary school. In all, how many children are in school?

   $4 + 9 = 13$

66   Brainy Book of Addition and Subtraction

Page 66

Shining Stars

Name _____

Add to find the sum.

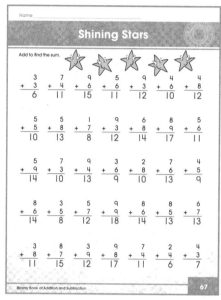

3 +3 = 6	7 +4 = 11	9 +6 = 15	5 +6 = 11	9 +3 = 12	4 +6 = 10	4 +8 = 12
5 +5 = 10	5 +8 = 13	1 +7 = 8	9 +3 = 12	6 +8 = 14	8 +9 = 17	5 +6 = 11
5 +9 = 14	7 +3 = 10	4 +9 = 13	3 +6 = 9	2 +8 = 10	7 +6 = 13	4 +5 = 9
8 +6 = 14	3 +5 = 8	5 +7 = 12	9 +9 = 18	8 +6 = 14	8 +5 = 13	6 +7 = 13
3 +8 = 11	8 +7 = 15	3 +9 = 12	9 +8 = 17	7 +4 = 11	2 +4 = 6	4 +3 = 7

Brainy Book of Addition and Subtraction   67

Page 67

Mystery Sums

Name _____

Add to find the sums.

2 +9 = 11	6 +6 = 12	4 +9 = 13	5 +4 = 9	5 +9 = 14	7 +7 = 14	3 +5 = 8
9 +9 = 18	5 +8 = 13	9 +8 = 17	6 +5 = 11	8 +5 = 13	9 +6 = 15	9 +4 = 13
4 +4 = 8	8 +6 = 14	9 +7 = 16	4 +6 = 10	5 +3 = 8	4 +5 = 9	9 +9 = 18
7 +3 = 10	6 +6 = 12	7 +8 = 15	3 +8 = 11	8 +3 = 11	4 +3 = 7	6 +7 = 13
3 +2 = 5	7 +5 = 12	3 +4 = 7	8 +8 = 16	5 +2 = 7	6 +3 = 9	2 +6 = 8

68   Brainy Book of Addition and Subtraction

Page 68

Time for Tens!

Name _____

Add the tens.

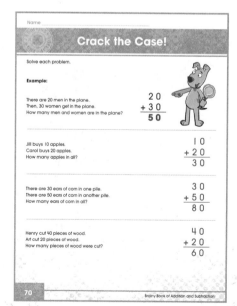

2 tens + 4 tens = 6 tens	6 tens + 2 tens = 8 tens

20 + 40 = 60	60 + 20 = 80	20 + 20 = 40	10 + 50 = 60
40 + 20 = 60	30 + 40 = 70	50 + 30 = 80	30 + 20 = 50
60 + 10 = 70	20 + 50 = 70	70 + 10 = 80	10 + 10 = 20
10 + 20 = 30	40 + 40 = 80	80 + 10 = 90	60 + 30 = 90	20 + 60 = 80

Brainy Book of Addition and Subtraction   69

Page 69

Crack the Case!

Name _____

Solve each problem.

Example:

There are 20 men in the plane. Then, 30 women get in the plane. How many men and women are in the plane?

$20 + 30 = 50$

Jill buys 10 apples. Carol buys 20 apples. How many apples in all?

$10 + 20 = 30$

There are 30 ears of corn in one pile. There are 50 ears of corn in another pile. How many ears of corn in all?

$30 + 50 = 80$

Henry cut 40 pieces of wood. Art cut 20 pieces of wood. How many pieces of wood were cut?

$40 + 20 = 60$

70   Brainy Book of Addition and Subtraction

Page 70

Answer Key

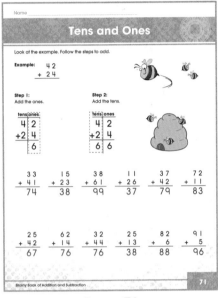

Page 71

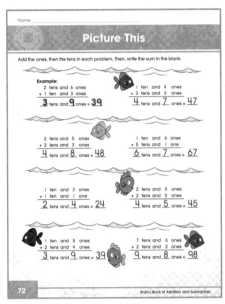

Page 72

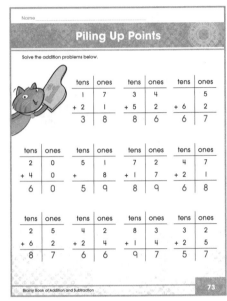

Page 73

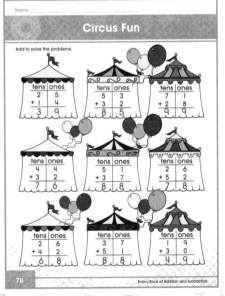

Page 74

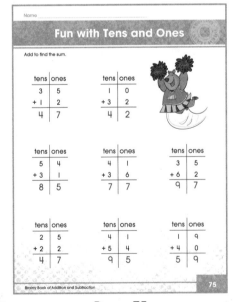

Page 75

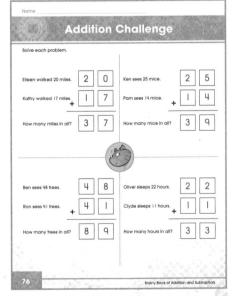

Page 76

Answer Key

Hungry for Honey

Write the answers to each problem to find the number of bees in each hive.
Use the letters to solve the riddle.

K: 26 + 13 = 39
M: 82 + 15 = 97
L: 12 + 32 = 44
E: 34 + 45 = 79
J: 92 + 6 = 98
R: 46 + 31 = 77
B: 61 + 22 = 83
A: 56 + 12 = 68
C: 70 + 15 = 85

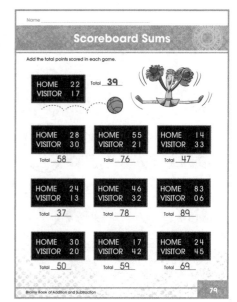

The honey was too hard to get, so Ted E. Bear ate something else. What was it?

B L A C K
83 44 68 85 39

" B E A R E "
83 79 68 77 79

J A M
98 68 97

Brainy Book of Addition and Subtraction 77

Page 77

Add It Up!

Solve each problem.

Ken sees 25 birds. — 2 5
Pilar sees 20 birds. + 2 0
How many birds in all? 4 5

Rachel has 88 marbles. — 8 8
Paul has 11 marbles. + 1 1
How many marbles in all? 9 9

Sam has 11 rabbits. — 1 1
Porchia has 25 rabbits. + 2 5
How many rabbits in all? 3 6

Jorge has 53 coins. — 5 3
Darrell has 36 coins. + 3 6
How many coins in all? 8 9

78 *Brainy Book of Addition and Subtraction*

Page 78

Scoreboard Sums

Add the total points scored in each game.

HOME 22 / VISITOR 17 — Total **39**

HOME 28 / VISITOR 30 — Total **58**
HOME 55 / VISITOR 21 — Total **76**
HOME 14 / VISITOR 33 — Total **47**

HOME 24 / VISITOR 13 — Total **37**
HOME 46 / VISITOR 32 — Total **78**
HOME 83 / VISITOR 06 — Total **89**

HOME 30 / VISITOR 20 — Total **50**
HOME 17 / VISITOR 42 — Total **59**
HOME 24 / VISITOR 45 — Total **69**

Brainy Book of Addition and Subtraction 79

Page 79

Find the 10s

Circle the two numbers in each row that equal 10. Then, write the third number in the number sentence with 10 and solve for the sum. The first one has been done for you.

12 + (9) + (1) = 10 + **12** = **22**

(7) + 26 + (3) = 10 + **26** = **36**

(2) + 90 + (8) = 10 + **90** = **100**

(5) + 86 + (5) = 10 + **86** = **96**

(6) + (4) + 31 = 10 + **31** = **41**

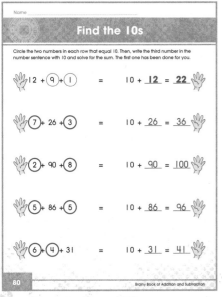

80 *Brainy Book of Addition and Subtraction*

Page 80

Find the 20s

Circle the two numbers in each row that equal 20. Then, write the third number in the number sentence with 20 and solve for the sum. The first one has been done for you.

12 + (18) + (2) = 20 + **12** = **32**

(17) + 26 + (3) = 20 + **26** = **46**

(8) + 80 + (12) = 20 + **80** = **100**

(10) + 97 + (10) = 20 + **97** = **117**

(14) + (6) + 41 = 20 + **41** = **61**

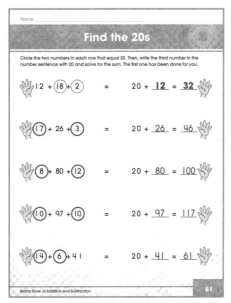

Brainy Book of Addition and Subtraction 81

Page 81

Add and Solve

Solve each problem.

Danny has 78 toys. — 7 8
Yasmin has 21 toys. + 2 1
How many toys in all? 9 9

Joanna has 11 puppies. — 1 1
Pablo has 37 puppies. + 3 7
How many puppies in all? 4 8

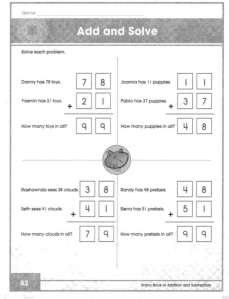

Rashawnda sees 38 clouds. — 3 8
Seth sees 41 clouds. + 4 1
How many clouds in all? 7 9

Randy has 48 pretzels. — 4 8
Sierra has 51 pretzels. + 5 1
How many pretzels in all? 9 9

82 *Brainy Book of Addition and Subtraction*

Page 82

Answer Key

Page 83

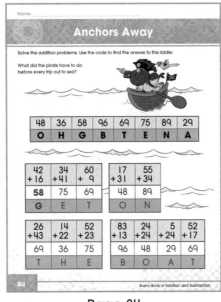

Page 84

Addition Challenge

Solve each problem.

Donna sees 38 cats.	3 8	Delinda has 10 ribbons.	1 0
Reba sees 61 cats.	+ 6 1	Stefanie has 12 ribbons.	+ 1 2
How many cats in all?	9 9	How many ribbons in all?	2 2

Chris has 29 pencils.	2 9	Khalil sees 73 people.	7 3
Bobbi has 40 pencils.	+ 4 0	Patrick sees 13 people.	+ 1 3
How many pencils in all?	6 9	How many people in all?	8 6

Page 85

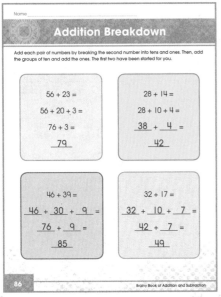

Page 86

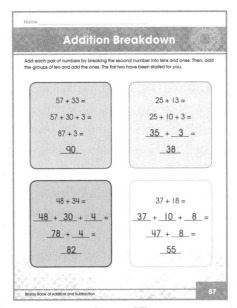

Page 87

Brain Power

Use mental math to find each sum. (Hint: Make tens or multiples of 10 first.) Then, write in the cloud how you solved each problem.

$12 + 5 + 8 + 5 = 30$

$31 + 7 + 3 = 41$

Written answers will vary.

$7 + 9 + 13 = 29$

$80 + 19 + 1 = 100$

I BET YOU'LL BE ABLE TO FIGURE THIS OUT!

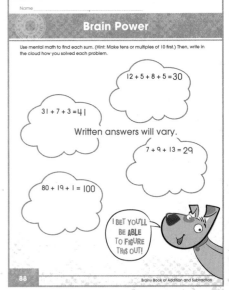

Page 88

Answer Key

Page 89

Brain Boost

Use mental math to find each sum. Then, write in the cloud how you solved each problem.

$41 + 8 + 2 = 51$

$13 + 4 + 7 + 4 = 28$

Written answers will vary.

SHOW ME HOW IT'S DONE!

$70 + 18 + 3 = 91$

$8 + 7 + 14 = 29$

Page 89

Page 90

Add It Up!

Solve each problem.

Ruby has 39 candles. | 3 9
Samir has 10 candles. | + 1 0
How many candles in all? | 4 9

Roberto sees 36 bugs. | 3 6
Doug sees 32 bugs. | + 3 2
How many bugs in all? | 6 8

Myong ran 10 miles. | 1 0
Dawn ran 13 miles. | + 1 3
How many miles in all? | 2 3

Greg has 31 bags. | 3 1
Rudy has 48 bags. | + 4 8
How many bags in all? | 7 9

Page 90

Page 91

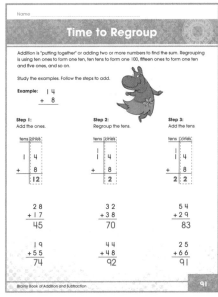

Time to Regroup

Addition is "putting together" or adding two or more numbers to find the sum. Regrouping is using ten ones to form one ten, ten tens to form one 100, fifteen ones to form one ten and five ones, and so on.

Study the examples. Follow the steps to add.

Example: 1 4
       + 8

Step 1: Add the ones.

tens	ones
1	4
+	8
	12

Step 2: Regroup the tens.

tens	ones
1	4
+	8
2	2

Step 3: Add the tens

tens	ones
1	4
+	8
2	2

$$28 + 17 = 45$$
$$32 + 38 = 70$$
$$54 + 29 = 83$$

$$19 + 55 = 74$$
$$44 + 48 = 92$$
$$25 + 66 = 91$$

Page 91

Page 92

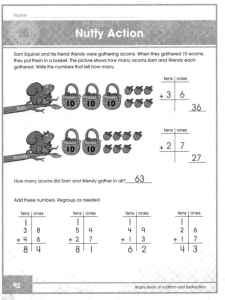

Nutty Action

Sam Squirrel and his friend Wendy were gathering acorns. When they gathered 10 acorns, they put them in a basket. The picture shows how many acorns Sam and Wendy each gathered. Write the numbers that tell how many.

Sam: tens ones + 3 6 = 36

Wendy: tens ones + 2 7 = 27

How many acorns did Sam and Wendy gather in all? **63**

Add these numbers. Regroup as needed.

tens	ones
1	
3	8
+ 4	6
8	4

tens	ones
5	4
+ 2	7
8	1

tens	ones
4	9
+ 1	3
6	2

tens	ones
1	
2	6
+ 1	7
4	3

Page 92

Page 93

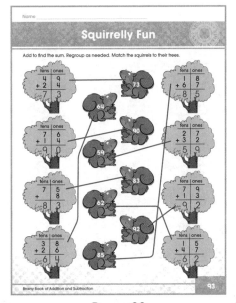

Squirrelly Fun

Add to find the sum. Regroup as needed. Match the squirrels to their trees.

tens ones: 4 9 + 2 4 = 73

tens ones: 7 6 + 1 4 = 90

tens ones: 7 5 + 1 3 = 88

tens ones: 3 8 + 2 6 = 64

tens ones: 1 8 + 6 7 = 85

tens ones: 2 7 + 3 2 = 59

tens ones: 7 9 + 1 3 = 92

tens ones: 1 5 + 4 7 = 62

Page 93

Page 94

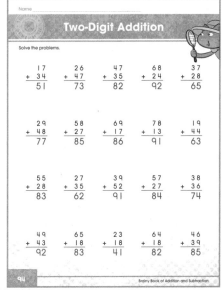

Two-Digit Addition

Solve the problems.

$$17 + 34 = 51$$
$$26 + 47 = 73$$
$$47 + 35 = 82$$
$$68 + 24 = 92$$
$$37 + 28 = 65$$

$$29 + 48 = 77$$
$$58 + 27 = 85$$
$$69 + 17 = 86$$
$$78 + 13 = 91$$
$$19 + 44 = 63$$

$$55 + 28 = 83$$
$$27 + 35 = 62$$
$$39 + 52 = 91$$
$$57 + 27 = 84$$
$$38 + 36 = 74$$

$$49 + 43 = 92$$
$$65 + 18 = 83$$
$$23 + 18 = 41$$
$$64 + 18 = 82$$
$$46 + 39 = 85$$

Page 94

Answer Key

Page 95

Solve the Problems!

Solve each problem.

Example:

16 boys ride their bikes to school.
18 girls ride their bikes to school.
How many bikes are ridden to school?

$$\begin{array}{r} 16 \\ +18 \\ \hline 34 \end{array}$$

Davis reads 26 pages.
Mike reads 37 pages.
How many pages did Davis and Mike read?

$$\begin{array}{r} 26 \\ +37 \\ \hline 63 \end{array}$$

Travon counts 46 stars.
Nina counts 39 stars.
How many stars did they count?

$$\begin{array}{r} 46 \\ +39 \\ \hline 85 \end{array}$$

Mom has 29 golf balls.
Dad has 43 golf balls.
How many golf balls do they have?

$$\begin{array}{r} 29 \\ +43 \\ \hline 72 \end{array}$$

Page 96

Shoot for the Stars

Add the total points scored in the game.

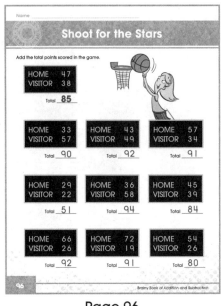

HOME 47 VISITOR 38 — Total **85**

HOME 33 VISITOR 57 — Total **90**
HOME 43 VISITOR 49 — Total **92**
HOME 57 VISITOR 34 — Total **91**

HOME 29 VISITOR 22 — Total **51**
HOME 36 VISITOR 58 — Total **94**
HOME 45 VISITOR 39 — Total **84**

HOME 66 VISITOR 26 — Total **92**
HOME 72 VISITOR 19 — Total **91**
HOME 54 VISITOR 26 — Total **80**

Page 97

Keep on Truckin'

Write each sum. Connect the sums of 83 to make a road for the truck.

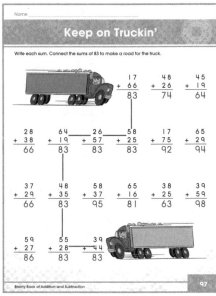

$$\begin{array}{r} 17 \\ +66 \\ \hline 83 \end{array} \quad \begin{array}{r} 48 \\ +26 \\ \hline 74 \end{array} \quad \begin{array}{r} 45 \\ +19 \\ \hline 64 \end{array}$$

$$\begin{array}{r} 28 \\ +38 \\ \hline 66 \end{array} \quad \begin{array}{r} 64 \\ +19 \\ \hline 83 \end{array} \quad \begin{array}{r} 26 \\ +57 \\ \hline 83 \end{array} \quad \begin{array}{r} 58 \\ +25 \\ \hline 83 \end{array} \quad \begin{array}{r} 17 \\ +75 \\ \hline 92 \end{array} \quad \begin{array}{r} 65 \\ +29 \\ \hline 94 \end{array}$$

$$\begin{array}{r} 37 \\ +29 \\ \hline 66 \end{array} \quad \begin{array}{r} 48 \\ +35 \\ \hline 83 \end{array} \quad \begin{array}{r} 58 \\ +37 \\ \hline 95 \end{array} \quad \begin{array}{r} 65 \\ +16 \\ \hline 81 \end{array} \quad \begin{array}{r} 38 \\ +25 \\ \hline 63 \end{array} \quad \begin{array}{r} 39 \\ +59 \\ \hline 98 \end{array}$$

$$\begin{array}{r} 59 \\ +27 \\ \hline 86 \end{array} \quad \begin{array}{r} 55 \\ +28 \\ \hline 83 \end{array} \quad \begin{array}{r} 39 \\ +44 \\ \hline 83 \end{array}$$

Page 98

Addition Challenge

Solve each problem.

Elijah has 29 hats.
Arifa has 52 hats.
How many hats in all?

$$\begin{array}{r} 5\ 9 \\ +\ 5\ 2 \\ \hline 8\ 1 \end{array}$$

Clarke has 73 cards.
Mandy has 25 cards.
How many cards in all?

$$\begin{array}{r} 7\ 3 \\ +\ 2\ 5 \\ \hline 9\ 8 \end{array}$$

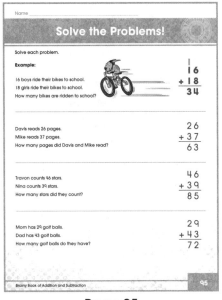

Ryan sees 14 kites.
Alexa sees 48 kites.
How many kites in all?

$$\begin{array}{r} 1\ 4 \\ +\ 4\ 8 \\ \hline 6\ 2 \end{array}$$

Paige sees 14 bikes.
Ben sees 39 bikes.
How many bikes in all?

$$\begin{array}{r} 1\ 4 \\ +\ 3\ 9 \\ \hline 5\ 3 \end{array}$$

Page 99

Just Like Magic

Add to find the sum.

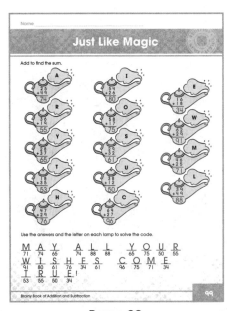

A 25 + 49 = 74
R 41 + 14 = 55
Y 28 + 37 = 65
T 35 + 18 = 53
H 47 + 29 = 76

I 54 + 26 = 80
O 58 + 17 = 75
S 29 + 32 = 61
U 12 + 38 = 50
C 87 + 9 = 96

E 17 + 17 = 34
W 62 + 29 = 91
M 27 + 44 = 71
L 39 + 49 = 88

Use the answers and the letter on each lamp to solve the code.

M A Y   A L L   Y O U R
71 74 65 74 88 88 65 75 71 34

W I S H E S   C O M E
80 80 61 76 34 61 96 75 71 34

T R U E !
53 55 50 34

Page 100

Subtraction 1, 2, 3

Practice writing the numbers and then subtract.

1 one
2 two
3 three

$$\begin{array}{r} 3 \\ -1 \\ \hline 2 \end{array} \quad \begin{array}{r} 4 \\ -3 \\ \hline 1 \end{array}$$

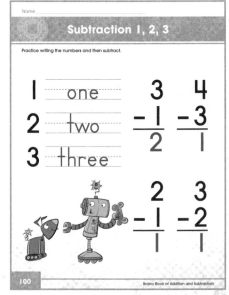

$$\begin{array}{r} 2 \\ -1 \\ \hline 1 \end{array} \quad \begin{array}{r} 3 \\ -2 \\ \hline 1 \end{array}$$

Answer Key

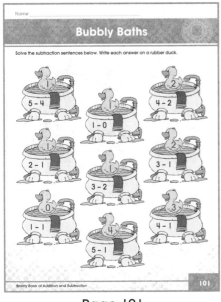

Page 101

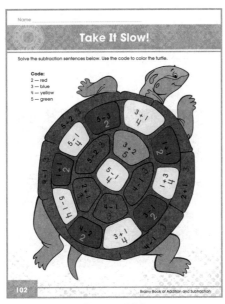

Page 102

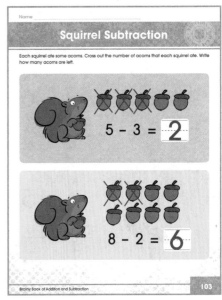

Page 103

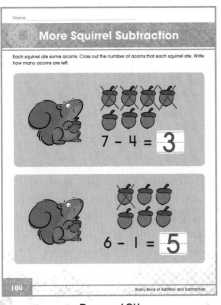

Page 104

Page 105

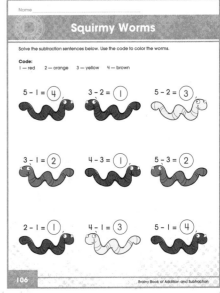

Page 106

Answer Key

Subtraction 4, 5, 6

Practice writing the numbers and then subtract. Draw dots and cross them out, if needed.

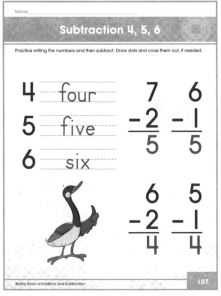

4 four
5 five
6 six

$$\begin{array}{r} 7 \\ -2 \\ \hline 5 \end{array} \quad \begin{array}{r} 6 \\ -1 \\ \hline 5 \end{array}$$

$$\begin{array}{r} 6 \\ -2 \\ \hline 4 \end{array} \quad \begin{array}{r} 5 \\ -1 \\ \hline 4 \end{array}$$

Page 107

"Berry" Tasty

Solve the subtraction sentences below. Use the code to color the picture.

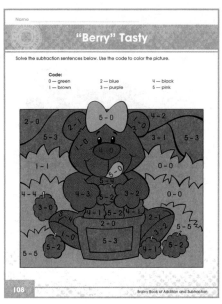

Code:
0 — green   2 — blue   4 — black
1 — brown   3 — purple   5 — pink

Page 108

Making a Splash!

Six silly green frogs were sitting on six lily pads.

A big bird flew by and two frogs jumped off into the water.

Solve the subtraction problem by answering the questions.

How many frogs were sitting on the lily pads? __6__

How many frogs jumped off? __2__

How many frogs were left? __4__

Page 109

Nutty Subtraction

Count the nuts in each dish. Write the answer on the line by each dish.
Circle the problems that equal the answer.

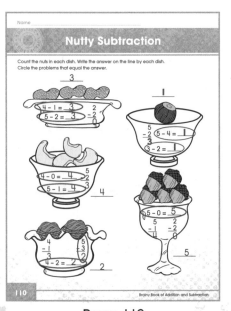

Page 110

Swamp Stories

Read the story. Subtract to find the difference. Write the number in the box.

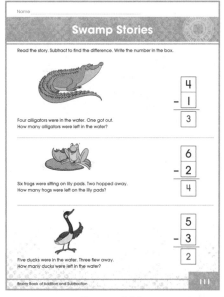

$$\begin{array}{r} 4 \\ -1 \\ \hline 3 \end{array}$$

Four alligators were in the water. One got out. How many alligators were left in the water?

$$\begin{array}{r} 6 \\ -2 \\ \hline 4 \end{array}$$

Six frogs were sitting on lily pads. Two hopped away. How many frogs were left on the lily pads?

$$\begin{array}{r} 5 \\ -3 \\ \hline 2 \end{array}$$

Five ducks were in the water. Three flew away. How many ducks were left in the water?

Page 111

Under the Sea

Complete the subtraction sentences.

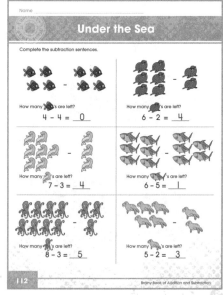

How many 's are left?
4 - 4 = 0

How many 's are left?
6 - 2 = 4

How many 's are left?
7 - 3 = 4

How many 's are left?
6 - 5 = 1

How many 's are left?
8 - 3 = 5

How many 's are left?
5 - 2 = 3

Page 112

Answer Key

Wheels and Wings

Complete the subtraction sentences.

$4 - 1 = \underline{3}$ $6 - 2 = \underline{4}$

$5 - 3 = \underline{2}$ $7 - 3 = \underline{4}$

$5 - 2 = \underline{3}$ $7 - 5 = \underline{2}$

Page 113

What's Left?

Complete the subtraction sentences.

$6 - 2 = \underline{4}$ $9 - 5 = \underline{4}$

$7 - 2 = \underline{5}$ $4 - 1 = \underline{3}$

$8 - 1 = \underline{7}$ $4 - 0 = \underline{4}$

Page 114

Take It Away!

Complete the subtraction sentences.

$5 - 2 = \underline{3}$ $6 - 1 = \underline{5}$

$7 - 4 = \underline{3}$ $8 - 3 = \underline{5}$

$9 - 2 = \underline{7}$ $4 - 4 = \underline{0}$

Page 115

A Whale of a Job!

Use fish crackers to subtract. Put the number of fish needed in the "water." Then, take them away by sliding them into the whale's mouth. Count how many fish are left.

$\begin{array}{r}7\\-3\\\hline4\end{array}$ $\begin{array}{r}9\\-2\\\hline7\end{array}$ $\begin{array}{r}6\\-4\\\hline2\end{array}$ $\begin{array}{r}5\\-2\\\hline3\end{array}$ $\begin{array}{r}8\\-3\\\hline5\end{array}$

$\begin{array}{r}9\\-3\\\hline6\end{array}$ $\begin{array}{r}6\\-3\\\hline3\end{array}$ $\begin{array}{r}7\\-5\\\hline2\end{array}$ $\begin{array}{r}8\\-2\\\hline6\end{array}$ $\begin{array}{r}5\\-1\\\hline4\end{array}$

$8 - 4 = \underline{4}$ $6 - 2 = \underline{4}$ $7 - 4 = \underline{3}$

Page 116

At the Bakery

Look at each number sentence. Find each missing number by circling the food items that are left over.

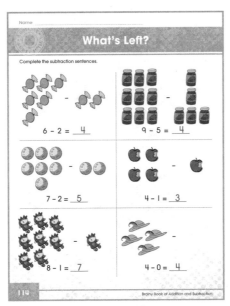

$5 - \underline{1} = 4$

$6 - \underline{2} = 4$

Page 117

Bake and Take

Look at each number sentence. Find each missing number by circling the food items that are left over.

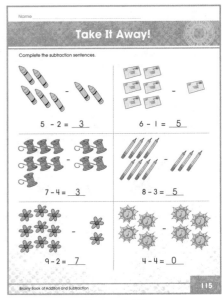

$7 - \underline{4} = 3$

$8 - \underline{6} = 2$

Page 118

Answer Key

Page 119

Page 120

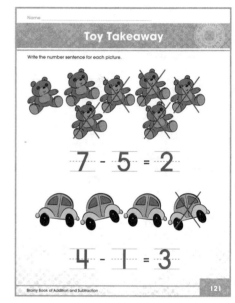

Page 121

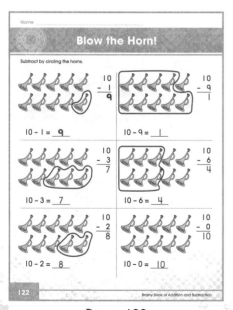

Page 122

Page 123

Page 124

Page 125

Name ___

How Many Left?

Solve each problem.

There are 10 white ❀
There are four blue ❀
How many more white ❀ than blue ❀ are there? **6**

$$\begin{array}{r} 10 \\ -\ 4 \\ \hline 6 \end{array}$$

Ten 🖍 are on the table.
Two are broken.
How many are not broken? **8**

$$\begin{array}{r} 10 \\ -\ 2 \\ \hline 8 \end{array}$$

There are nine 🐟
Six swim away.
How many 🐟 are left? **3**

$$\begin{array}{r} 9 \\ -\ 6 \\ \hline 3 \end{array}$$

Joni wants nine 🪙
She has five 🪙
How many more does she need? **4**

$$\begin{array}{r} 9 \\ -\ 5 \\ \hline 4 \end{array}$$

There were 10 ☃
Five ☃ melted.
How many did not melt? **5**

$$\begin{array}{r} 10 \\ -\ 5 \\ \hline 5 \end{array}$$

Brainy Book of Addition and Subtraction   125

Page 126

Name ___

Sweet Treats

Count the candy in each dish. Write the number on the line by each dish. Circle the problems that equal the answer.

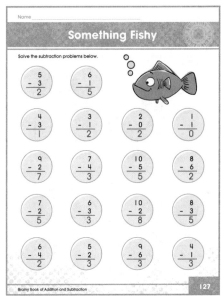

$7 - 1 = 6$
$\begin{array}{r} 8 \\ -\ 2 \\ \hline 6 \end{array}$
6

$10 - 1 = 9$
$10 - 4 = 6$
$\begin{array}{r} 9 \\ -\ 1 \\ \hline 8 \end{array}$
9

$\begin{array}{r} 8 \\ -\ 1 \\ \hline 7 \end{array}$
$0 - 3 = 7$
7

$\begin{array}{r} 10 \\ -\ 4 \\ \hline 6 \end{array}$
$\begin{array}{r} 8 \\ -\ 2 \\ \hline 6 \end{array}$
$7 - 2 = 5$
6

$\begin{array}{r} 9 \\ -\ 4 \\ \hline 5 \end{array}$
$\begin{array}{r} 9 \\ -\ 1 \\ \hline 8 \end{array}$
$7 - 2 = 5$
8

126   Brainy Book of Addition and Subtraction

Page 127

Name ___

Something Fishy

Solve the subtraction problems below.

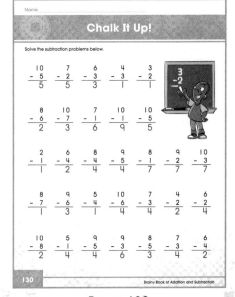

$\begin{array}{r} 5 \\ -\ 3 \\ \hline 2 \end{array}$
$\begin{array}{r} 6 \\ -\ 1 \\ \hline 5 \end{array}$

$\begin{array}{r} 4 \\ -\ 3 \\ \hline 1 \end{array}$
$\begin{array}{r} 3 \\ -\ 1 \\ \hline 2 \end{array}$
$\begin{array}{r} 2 \\ -\ 0 \\ \hline 2 \end{array}$
$\begin{array}{r} 1 \\ -\ 1 \\ \hline 0 \end{array}$

$\begin{array}{r} 9 \\ -\ 2 \\ \hline 7 \end{array}$
$\begin{array}{r} 7 \\ -\ 4 \\ \hline 3 \end{array}$
$\begin{array}{r} 10 \\ -\ 5 \\ \hline 5 \end{array}$
$\begin{array}{r} 8 \\ -\ 6 \\ \hline 2 \end{array}$

$\begin{array}{r} 7 \\ -\ 2 \\ \hline 5 \end{array}$
$\begin{array}{r} 6 \\ -\ 3 \\ \hline 3 \end{array}$
$\begin{array}{r} 10 \\ -\ 2 \\ \hline 8 \end{array}$
$\begin{array}{r} 8 \\ -\ 3 \\ \hline 5 \end{array}$

$\begin{array}{r} 6 \\ -\ 4 \\ \hline 2 \end{array}$
$\begin{array}{r} 5 \\ -\ 2 \\ \hline 3 \end{array}$
$\begin{array}{r} 9 \\ -\ 6 \\ \hline 3 \end{array}$
$\begin{array}{r} 4 \\ -\ 1 \\ \hline 3 \end{array}$

Brainy Book of Addition and Subtraction   127

Page 128

Name ___

Frogs on a Log

Roll a die. Starting at 10, count back the rolled number as hops on the log. Write what you did as a subtraction fact. Repeat four more times.

Answers will vary.

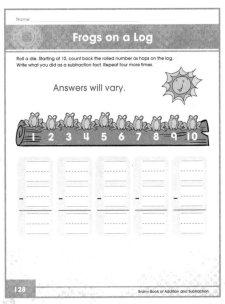

128   Brainy Book of Addition and Subtraction

Page 129

Name ___

Secrets of Subtraction

Solve the subtraction problems. Use the code to find the secret message.

Code:

7	5	2	6	4	3
K	T	Y	E	W	A

PLEASE, DON'T EVER

$\begin{array}{r}8\\-3\end{array}$	$\begin{array}{r}10\\-7\end{array}$	$\begin{array}{r}9\\-2\end{array}$	$\begin{array}{r}10\\-4\end{array}$		$\begin{array}{r}9\\-6\end{array}$	$\begin{array}{r}6\\-2\end{array}$	$\begin{array}{r}7\\-4\end{array}$	$\begin{array}{r}8\\-6\end{array}$
5	3	7	6		3	4	3	2
T	A	K	E		A	W	A	Y

MY MATH!

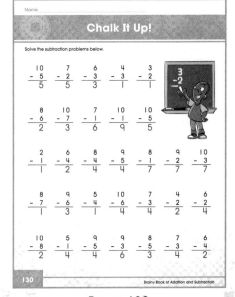

129

Page 130

Name ___

Chalk It Up!

Solve the subtraction problems below.

$\begin{array}{r} 10 \\ -\ 5 \\ \hline 5 \end{array}$
$\begin{array}{r} 7 \\ -\ 2 \\ \hline 5 \end{array}$
$\begin{array}{r} 6 \\ -\ 3 \\ \hline 3 \end{array}$
$\begin{array}{r} 4 \\ -\ 3 \\ \hline 1 \end{array}$
$\begin{array}{r} 3 \\ -\ 2 \\ \hline 1 \end{array}$

$\begin{array}{r} 8 \\ -\ 6 \\ \hline 2 \end{array}$
$\begin{array}{r} 10 \\ -\ 7 \\ \hline 3 \end{array}$
$\begin{array}{r} 7 \\ -\ 1 \\ \hline 6 \end{array}$
$\begin{array}{r} 10 \\ -\ 1 \\ \hline 9 \end{array}$
$\begin{array}{r} 10 \\ -\ 5 \\ \hline 5 \end{array}$

$\begin{array}{r} 2 \\ -\ 1 \\ \hline 1 \end{array}$
$\begin{array}{r} 6 \\ -\ 4 \\ \hline 2 \end{array}$
$\begin{array}{r} 8 \\ -\ 4 \\ \hline 4 \end{array}$
$\begin{array}{r} 9 \\ -\ 5 \\ \hline 4 \end{array}$
$\begin{array}{r} 9 \\ -\ 2 \\ \hline 7 \end{array}$
$\begin{array}{r} 10 \\ -\ 3 \\ \hline 7 \end{array}$

$\begin{array}{r} 8 \\ -\ 7 \\ \hline 1 \end{array}$
$\begin{array}{r} 9 \\ -\ 6 \\ \hline 3 \end{array}$
$\begin{array}{r} 5 \\ -\ 4 \\ \hline 1 \end{array}$
$\begin{array}{r} 10 \\ -\ 6 \\ \hline 4 \end{array}$
$\begin{array}{r} 7 \\ -\ 3 \\ \hline 4 \end{array}$
$\begin{array}{r} 4 \\ -\ 2 \\ \hline 2 \end{array}$
$\begin{array}{r} 6 \\ -\ 4 \\ \hline 2 \end{array}$

$\begin{array}{r} 10 \\ -\ 8 \\ \hline 2 \end{array}$
$\begin{array}{r} 5 \\ -\ 1 \\ \hline 4 \end{array}$
$\begin{array}{r} 9 \\ -\ 5 \\ \hline 4 \end{array}$
$\begin{array}{r} 9 \\ -\ 3 \\ \hline 6 \end{array}$
$\begin{array}{r} 8 \\ -\ 5 \\ \hline 3 \end{array}$
$\begin{array}{r} 7 \\ -\ 3 \\ \hline 4 \end{array}$
$\begin{array}{r} 6 \\ -\ 4 \\ \hline 2 \end{array}$

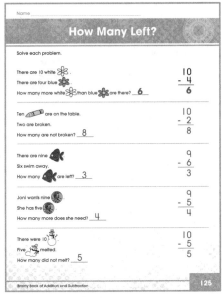

130   Brainy Book of Addition and Subtraction

Answer Key

Page 131

Crayon Count

Count the crayons. Write the number on the blank. Circle the problems that equal the answer.

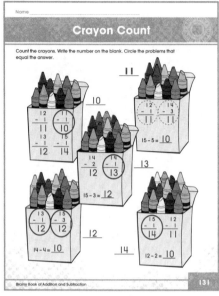

11

10

- 12 - 11
- -1 - -1
- 11 10

- -1 - -3
- 11 11

15 - 5 = 10

- 12 - 15
- -1 - -1
- 12 14

- 14 - 14
- -2 - -1
- 12 13

13

15 - 3 = 12

- 13 - 13
- -1 - -3
- 12 12

- 15 - 12
- -1 - -1
- 14 11

12

12

14 - 4 = 10

14

12 - 2 = 10

Brainy Book of Addition and Subtraction   131

Page 132

Subtraction Challenge

Solve each problem.

Kenyon sees 18 birds. 1 8

3 fly away. — 3

How many birds are left? 1 5

Carlos sees 19 snails. 1 9

Trey takes 6 snails. — 6

How many snails are left? 1 3

Kelsey has 18 ribbons. 1 8

She loses 7 ribbons. — 7

How many ribbons are left? 1 1

Braden has 17 cards. 1 7

He gives 2 away. — 2

How many cards are left? 1 5

132   Brainy Book of Addition and Subtraction

Page 133

Fun Facts

Solve the subtraction problems below.

- 16 - 14 - 17
- -9 - -7 - -9
- 7   7   8

- 14 - 15 - 16 - 12
- -8 - -8 - -8 - -3
- 6   7   8   9

- 14 - 18 - 15 - 13
- -9 - -9 - -9 - -7
- 5   9   6   6

- 16 - 15 - 13 - 12
- -8 - -8 - -8 - -4
- 8   7   5   8

- 14 - 13 - 16 - 13
- -6 - -3 - -7 - -9
- 8   10   9   4

Brainy Book of Addition and Subtraction   133

Page 134

How Many Are Left?

Solve each problem.

Taylor has 19 kites. 1 9

She gives 7 away. — 7

How many kites are left? 1 2

Spencer has 14 pencils. 1 4

1 pencil breaks. — 1

How many pencils are left? 1 3

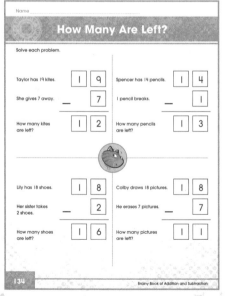

Lily has 18 shoes. 1 8

Her sister takes 2 shoes. — 2

How many shoes are left? 1 6

Colby draws 18 pictures. 1 8

He erases 7 pictures. — 7

How many pictures are left? 1 1

134   Brainy Book of Addition and Subtraction

Page 135

Three in a Row

Solve each subtraction problem. Then, draw a line to connect the three answers in each row that are the same.

12 - 9 = 3	11 - 2 = 9	9 - 8 = 1	10 - 7 = 3	12 - 3 = 9	11 - 2 = 9
8 - 6 = 2	7 - 4 = 3	7 - 5 = 2	12 - 7 = 5	9 - 0 = 9	8 - 5 = 3
7 - 3 = 4	10 - 1 = 9	11 - 8 = 3	11 - 4 = 7	9 - 2 = 7	12 - 5 = 7

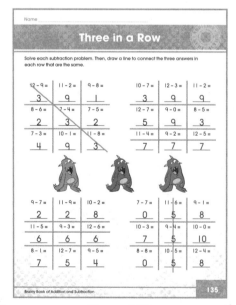

9 - 7 = 2	11 - 9 = 2	10 - 2 = 8	7 - 7 = 0	11 - 6 = 5	9 - 1 = 8
11 - 5 = 6	9 - 3 = 6	12 - 6 = 6	10 - 3 = 7	9 - 4 = 5	10 - 0 = 10
8 - 1 = 7	12 - 7 = 5	9 - 5 = 4	8 - 8 = 0	10 - 5 = 5	12 - 4 = 8

Brainy Book of Addition and Subtraction   135

Page 136

Subtract and Solve

Solve each problem.

Chelsea sees 16 planes. 1 6

7 planes take off. — 7

How many planes are left? 9

Sam has 17 marbles. 1 7

He loses 8 at school. — 8

How many marbles are left? 9

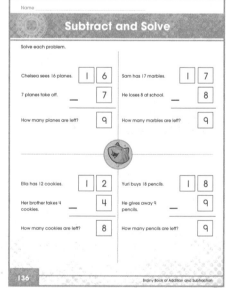

Ella has 12 cookies. 1 2

Her brother takes 4 cookies. — 4

How many cookies are left? 8

Yuri buys 18 pencils. 1 8

He gives away 9 pencils. — 9

How many pencils are left? 9

136   Brainy Book of Addition and Subtraction

Answer Key

Page 137

Play Ball!

Solve the problems.

Example:

| 13 − 5 = **8** | 14 − 9 = 5 |
| 14 − 8 = 6 | 13 − 4 = 9 |

12 − 7 = 5	10 − 2 = 8	13 − 4 = 9	14 − 9 = 5	11 − 8 = 3	14 − 5 = 9
14 − 6 = 8	12 − 8 = 4	13 − 5 = 8	10 − 6 = 4	13 − 6 = 7	13 − 7 = 6
11 − 6 = 5	13 − 9 = 4	14 − 8 = 6	12 − 3 = 9	14 − 7 = 7	13 − 8 = 5

Page 138

School Subtraction

Solve the problems.

Example:

| 15 − 7 = **8** | 16 − 9 = 7 |
| 17 − 8 = 9 | 18 − 9 = 9 |

18 − 9 = 9	13 − 5 = 8	16 − 8 = 8	17 − 9 = 8	14 − 6 = 8	13 − 9 = 4
17 − 8 = 9	15 − 9 = 6	14 − 5 = 9	13 − 6 = 7	16 − 7 = 9	12 − 4 = 8
14 − 7 = 7	15 − 8 = 7	16 − 9 = 7	12 − 7 = 5	15 − 7 = 8	13 − 4 = 9

Page 139

Subtraction Challenge

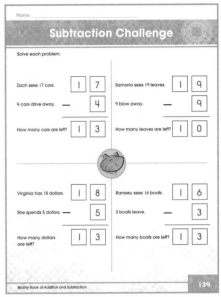

Solve each problem.

Zach sees 17 cars. 17
4 cars drive away. − 4
How many cars are left? 13

Samaria sees 19 leaves. 19
9 blow away. − 9
How many leaves are left? 10

Virginia has 18 dollars. 18
She spends 5 dollars. − 5
How many dollars are left? 13

Ramsey sees 16 boats. 16
3 boats leave. − 3
How many boats are left? 13

Page 140

How Many More?

Count the gumballs in the pair of gumball machines. Write a number sentence to show how many more gumballs are in the first machine.

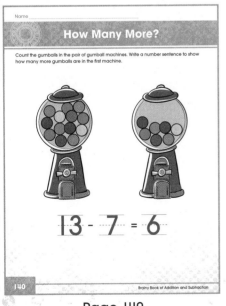

13 − 7 = 6

Page 141

Gumballs Galore

Count the gumballs in the pair of gumball machines. Write a number sentence to show how many more gumballs are in the first machine.

11 − 6 = 5

Page 142

Subtract and Solve

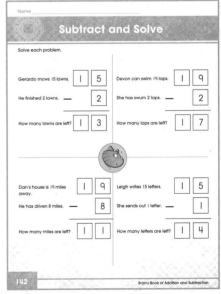

Solve each problem.

Gerardo mows 15 lawns. 15
He finished 2 lawns. − 2
How many lawns are left? 13

Devon can swim 19 laps. 19
She has swum 2 laps. − 2
How many laps are left? 17

Dan's house is 19 miles away. 19
He has driven 8 miles. − 8
How many miles are left? 11

Leigh writes 15 letters. 15
She sends out 1 letter. − 1
How many letters are left? 14

Page 143

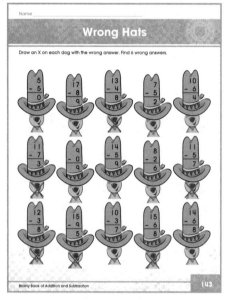

Wrong Hats

Draw an X on each dog with the wrong answer. Find 6 wrong answers.

Page 144

Big Cat!

Subtract. Write the answer in the space. Then, color the spaces according to the answers.

Code:
1 — white 2 — purple 3 — black 4 — green 5 — yellow
6 — blue 7 — pink 8 — gray 9 — orange 10 — red

Page 145

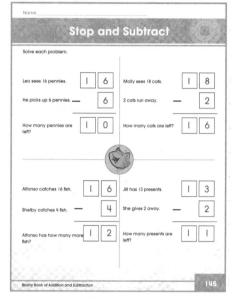

Stop and Subtract

Solve each problem.

Leo sees 16 pennies.	1 6		Molly sees 18 cats.	1 8
He picks up 6 pennies.	6		2 cats run away.	2
How many pennies are left?	1 0		How many cats are left?	1 6

Alfonso catches 16 fish.	1 6		Jill has 13 presents.	1 3
Shelby catches 4 fish.	4		She gives 2 away.	2
Alfonso has how many more fish?	1 2		How many presents are left?	1 1

Page 146

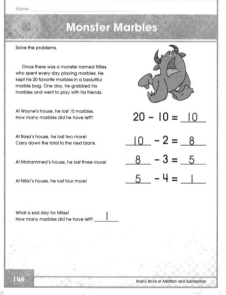

Monster Marbles

Solve the problems.

Once there was a monster named Miles who spent every day playing marbles. He kept his 20 favorite marbles in a beautiful marble bag. One day, he grabbed his marbles and went to play with his friends.

At Wayne's house, he lost 10 marbles. How many marbles did he have left?

$20 - 10 = \underline{10}$

At Rosa's house, he lost two more! Carry down the total to the next blank.

$\underline{10} - 2 = \underline{8}$

At Mohammed's house, he lost three more!

$\underline{8} - 3 = \underline{5}$

At Nikki's house, he lost four more!

$\underline{5} - 4 = \underline{1}$

What a sad day for Miles! How many marbles did he have left? $\underline{1}$

Page 147

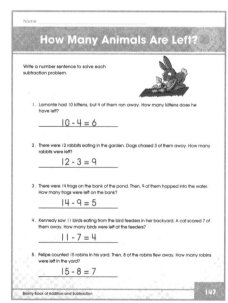

How Many Animals Are Left?

Write a number sentence to solve each subtraction problem.

1. Lamonte had 10 kittens, but 4 of them ran away. How many kittens does he have left?

$10 - 4 = 6$

2. There were 12 rabbits eating in the garden. Dogs chased 3 of them away. How many rabbits were left?

$12 - 3 = 9$

3. There were 14 frogs on the bank of the pond. Then, 9 of them hopped into the water. How many frogs were left on the bank?

$14 - 9 = 5$

4. Kennedy saw 11 birds eating from the bird feeders in her backyard. A cat scared 7 of them away. How many birds were left at the feeders?

$11 - 7 = 4$

5. Felipe counted 15 robins in his yard. Then, 8 of the robins flew away. How many robins were left in the yard?

$15 - 8 = 7$

Page 148

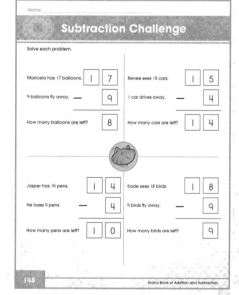

Subtraction Challenge

Solve each problem.

Maricela has 17 balloons.	1 7		Renee sees 15 cars.	1 5
9 balloons fly away.	9		1 car drives away.	4
How many balloons are left?	8		How many cars are left?	1 4

Jasper has 14 pens.	1 4		Kade sees 18 birds.	1 8
He loses 4 pens.	4		9 birds fly away.	9
How many pens are left?	1 0		How many birds are left?	9

Answer Key

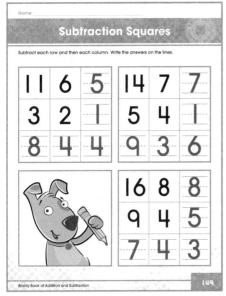

Page 149

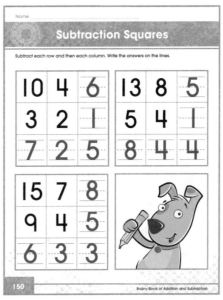

Page 150

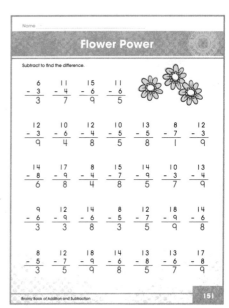

Page 151

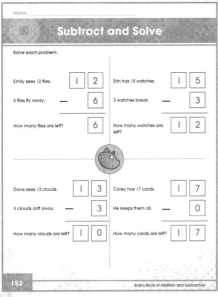

Page 152

Page 153

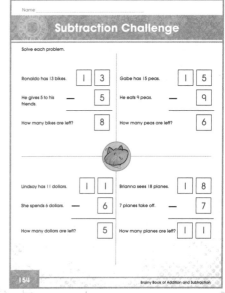

Page 154

Answer Key

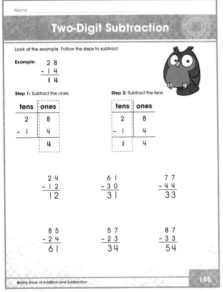

Page 155

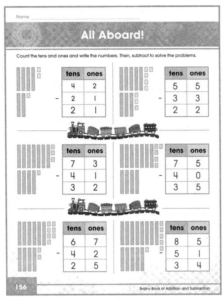

Page 156

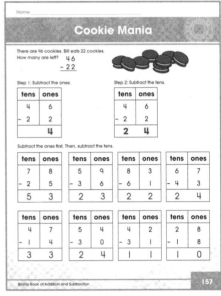

Page 157

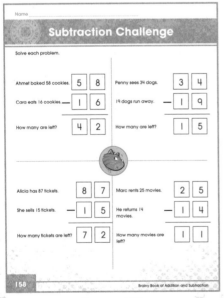

Page 158

Page 159

Page 160

Page 161

How Many Are Left?

Solve the problems.

Alvin has 89 dollars.	8 9	The pond has 64 fish.	6 4
He spends 72 dollars. −	7 2	Temille catches 24 fish. −	2 4
How many dollars are left?	1 7	How many are left?	4 0

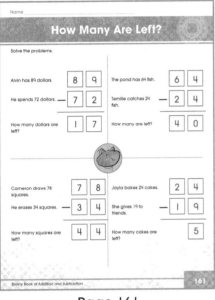

Cameron draws 78 squares.	7 8	Jayla bakes 24 cakes.	2 4
He erases 34 squares. −	3 4	She gives 19 to friends. −	1 9
How many squares are left?	4 4	How many cakes are left?	5

161

Brainy Book of Addition and Subtraction

Page 162

Mystery Numbers

Find the missing number behind each magnifying lens. Write a number sentence to solve for the missing number. Then, write the answer.

$$77 - \_\_ = 70$$
$$77 - 70 = 7$$
$$\_\_ = 7$$

$$29 - \_\_ = 17$$
$$29 - 17 = 12$$
$$\_\_ = 12$$

162   Brainy Book of Addition and Subtraction

Page 163

Digit Detective

Find the missing number behind each magnifying lens. Write a number sentence to solve for the missing number. Then, write the answer.

$$21 - \_\_ = 10$$
$$21 - 10 = 11$$
$$\_\_ = 11$$

$$37 - \_\_ = 15$$
$$37 - 15 = 22$$
$$\_\_ = 22$$

Brainy Book of Addition and Subtraction   163

Page 164

Subtraction Challenge

Solve each problem.

Lonnie sees 68 bugs.	6 8	Myra writes 95 letters.	9 5
52 bugs crawl away. −	5 2	She sends out 74 letters. −	7 4
How many bugs are left?	1 6	How many letters are left?	2 1

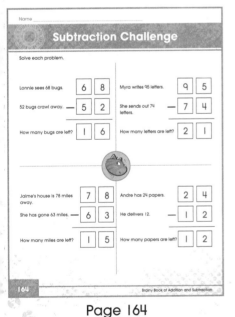

Jaime's house is 78 miles away.	7 8	Andre has 24 papers.	2 4
She has gone 63 miles. −	6 3	He delivers 12. −	1 2
How many miles are left?	1 5	How many papers are left?	1 2

164   Brainy Book of Addition and Subtraction

Page 165

Lion's Lunch

Leon the Lion was very hungry. Write the answers to the problems to find out how many bones he ate. Circle all the differences that are smaller than 20.

56 − 42 = (14)	39 − 18 = 21	44 − 21 = 23	26 − 13 = (13)	67 − 35 = 32
88 − 15 = 73	79 − 58 = 21	59 − 28 = 31	68 − 47 = 21	94 − 83 = (11)
32 − 21 = (11)	56 − 15 = 41	86 − 23 = 63	74 − 31 = 43	66 − 52 = (14)

Brainy Book of Addition and Subtraction   165

Page 166

Cookie Craze!

Subtract to solve the problems. Circle the answers. Color the cookies with answers greater than 30.

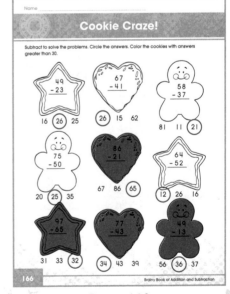

| 49 − 23 | 67 − 41 | 58 − 37 |
| 16 (26) 25 | (26) 15 62 | 81 11 (21) |

| 75 − 50 | 86 − 21 | 64 − 52 |
| 20 (25) 35 | 67 86 (65) | (12) 26 16 |

| 97 − 65 | 77 − 43 | 49 − 13 |
| 31 33 (32) | (34) 43 39 | 56 (36) 37 |

166   Brainy Book of Addition and Subtraction

Answer Key

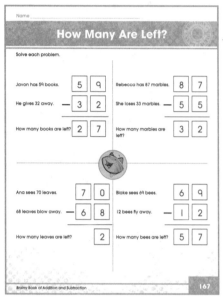

Page 167

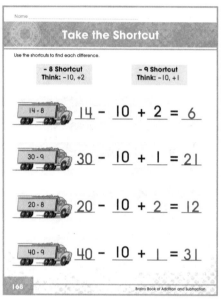

Page 168

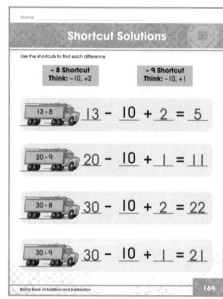

Page 169

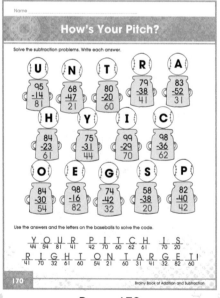

Page 170

Page 171

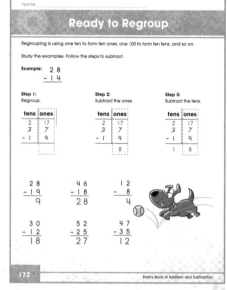

Page 172

Page 173

Two-Digit Subtraction

Solve the problems.

63 − 48 = 15	83 − 45 = 38	74 − 29 = 45	94 − 48 = 46	62 − 25 = 37
45 − 27 = 18	33 − 24 = 9	24 − 8 = 16	86 − 37 = 49	72 − 48 = 24
36 − 17 = 19	26 − 18 = 8	43 − 19 = 24	63 − 48 = 15	93 − 18 = 75
82 − 26 = 56	73 − 28 = 45	95 − 69 = 26	57 − 38 = 19	41 − 25 = 16

Page 174

What's the Difference?

Solve each problem.

tens	ones		tens	ones		tens	ones
5	4		3	3		6	1
− 1	7		− 1	5		− 3	3
3	7		1	8		2	8

tens	ones		tens	ones		tens	ones
2	7		4	2		5	2
− 1	6		− 2	4		− 2	6
1	1		1	8		2	6

tens	ones		tens	ones		tens	ones
9	4		7	7		6	5
− 4	8		− 3	4		− 2	6
4	6		4	3		3	9

Page 175

Subtraction Challenge

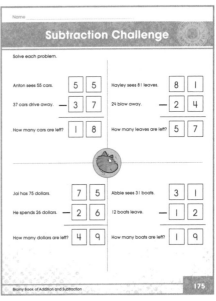

Solve each problem.

Anton sees 55 cars. [5][5]
37 cars drive away. − [3][7]
How many cars are left? [1][8]

Hayley sees 81 leaves. [8][1]
24 blow away. − [2][4]
How many leaves are left? [5][7]

Jai has 75 dollars. [7][5]
He spends 26 dollars. − [2][6]
How many dollars are left? [4][9]

Abbie sees 31 boats. [3][1]
12 boats leave. − [1][2]
How many boats are left? [1][9]

Page 176

Undersea Adventure

Solve the subtraction problems below.

tens	ones		tens	ones		tens	ones
4	7		6	4		5	3
− 2	8		− 3	4		− 3	9
1	9		3	0		1	4

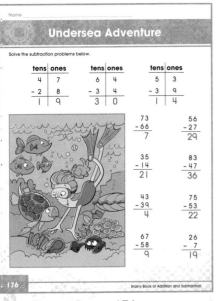

73 − 66 = 7	56 − 27 = 29
35 − 14 = 21	83 − 47 = 36
43 − 39 = 4	75 − 53 = 22
67 − 58 = 9	26 − 7 = 19

Page 177

Subtract and Solve

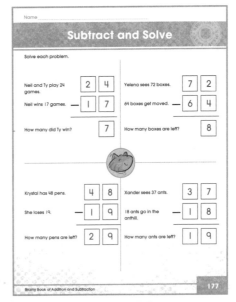

Solve each problem.

Neil and Ty play 24 games. [2][4]
Neil wins 17 games. − [1][7]
How many did Ty win? [7]

Yelena sees 72 boxes. [7][2]
64 boxes get moved. − [6][4]
How many boxes are left? [8]

Krystal has 48 pens. [4][8]
She loses 19. − [1][9]
How many pens are left? [2][9]

Xander sees 37 ants. [3][7]
18 ants go in the anthill. − [1][8]
How many ants are left? [1][9]

Page 178

Square Subtraction

Use the hundred board to solve each problem. Circle the first number in the problem on the board. Then, draw a path on the board as you count back to subtract the second number. Draw a triangle around the answer. Write the answer to complete the number sentence.

22 − 11 = __11__   67 − 14 = __53__   36 − 9 = __27__

88 − 12 = __76__   94 − 5 = __89__   51 − 12 = __39__

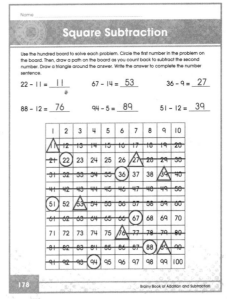

Answer Key

Square Subtraction

Use the hundred board to solve each problem. Circle the first number in the problem on the board. Then, draw a path on the board as you count back to subtract the second number. Draw a triangle around the answer. Write the answer to complete the number sentence.

31 - 10 = 21   57 - 13 = 44   19 - 8 = 11

77 - 12 = 65   99 - 6 = 93   88 - 10 = 78

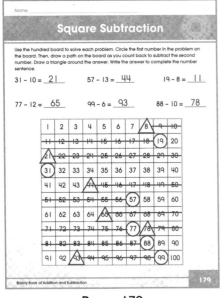

Page 179

Problem Solving

Write a number sentence to solve each problem.

Example:

Dad cooks 23 potatoes.
He used 19 potatoes in the potato salad.
How many potatoes are left?

23 - 19 = 4

Susan draws 32 butterflies.
She colors 15 of them brown.
How many butterflies does she have left to color?

32 - 15 = 17

A book has 66 pages.
Pedro reads 39 pages.
How many pages are left to read?

66 - 39 = 27

Jerry picks up 34 sea shells.
He puts 15 of them in a box.
How many does he have left?

34 - 15 = 19

Page 180

Subtraction Challenge

Solve each problem.

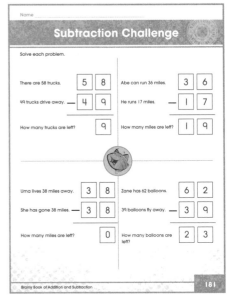

There are 58 trucks. [5] [8]
49 trucks drive away. [4] [9]
How many trucks are left? [9]

Abe can run 36 miles. [3] [6]
He runs 17 miles. — [1] [7]
How many miles are left? [1] [9]

Uma lives 38 miles away. [3] [8]
She has gone 38 miles. — [3] [8]
How many miles are left? [0]

Zane has 62 balloons. [6] [2]
39 balloons fly away. — [3] [9]
How many balloons are left? [2] [3]

Page 181

A Day at the Beach

Subtract to find the difference. Regroup as needed. Color the spaces with differences of:

10 — 19: red   50 — 59: brown   30 — 39: green
40 — 49: yellow   20 — 29: blue   60 — 69: orange

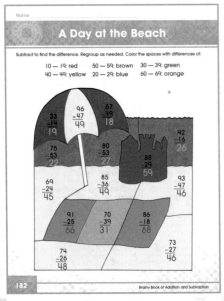

Page 182

Add or Subtract?

Write + or - in the circles. Then, solve the problems.

1. The pet store has 3 large dogs and 5 small dogs. How many dogs are there in all?

3 (+) 5 = 8

2. The pet store had 9 parrots and then sold 4 of them. How many parrots does the pet store have left?

9 (-) 4 = 5

3. At the pet store, 3 of the 8 kittens were sold. How many kittens are left in the pet store?

8 (-) 3 = 5

4. The pet store gave Linda's class 2 adult gerbils and 9 young ones. How many gerbils did Linda's class get in all?

2 (+) 9 = 11

5. The monkey at the pet store has 5 rubber toys and 4 wooden toys. How many toys does the monkey have in all?

5 (+) 4 = 9

Page 183

Wings and Water

Draw a line under the question that matches the picture. Then, solve the problems.

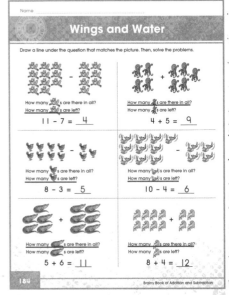

How many 🦋s are there in all?
How many 🦋s are left?
11 - 7 = 4

How many 🐙s are there in all?
How many 🐙s are left?
4 + 5 = 9

How many 🐔s are there in all?
How many 🐔s are left?
8 - 3 = 5

How many 🐟s are there in all?
How many 🐟s are left?
10 - 4 = 6

How many 🦐s are there in all?
How many 🦐s are left?
5 + 6 = 11

How many 🦐s are there in all?
How many 🦐s are left?
8 + 4 = 12

Page 184

Answer Key

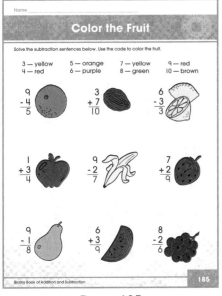

Page 185

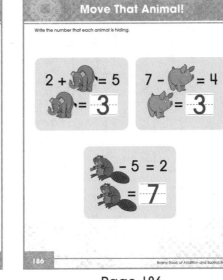

Page 186

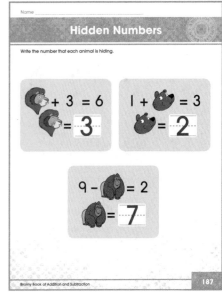

Page 187

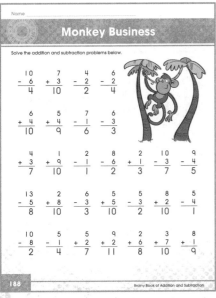

Page 188

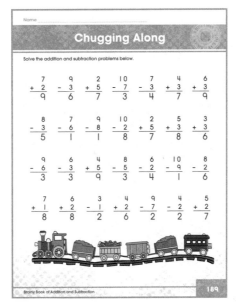

Page 189

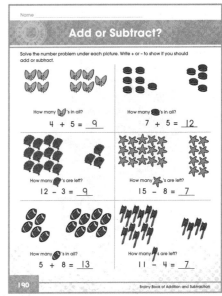

Page 190

Answer Key

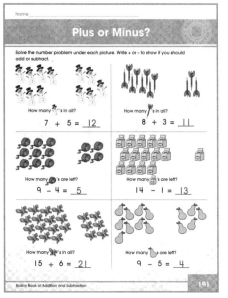

Plus or Minus?

Solve the number problem under each picture. Write + or − to show if you should add or subtract.

How many ☃'s in all?

$7 + 5 = 12$

How many 🎯's in all?

$8 + 3 = 11$

How many 🫐's are left?

$9 - 4 = 5$

How many 🍯's are left?

$14 - 1 = 13$

How many 🐝's in all?

$15 + 6 = 21$

How many 🍐's are left?

$9 - 5 = 4$

Brainy Book of Addition and Subtraction   191

Page 191

Blastoff Facts

Write the four facts for each fact family.

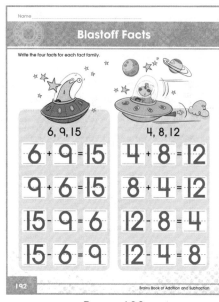

6, 9, 15

$6 + 9 = 15$

$9 + 6 = 15$

$15 - 9 = 6$

$15 - 6 = 9$

4, 8, 12

$4 + 8 = 12$

$8 + 4 = 12$

$12 - 8 = 4$

$12 - 4 = 8$

192   Brainy Book of Addition and Subtraction

Page 192

More Blastoff Facts

Write the four facts for each fact family.

6, 7, 13

$6 + 7 = 13$

$7 + 6 = 13$

$13 - 7 = 6$

$13 - 6 = 7$

8, 9, 17

$8 + 9 = 17$

$9 + 8 = 17$

$17 - 9 = 8$

$17 - 8 = 9$

Brainy Book of Addition and Subtraction   193

Page 193

Crazy Quilt

Solve the problems. From your answers, use the code to color the quilt.

6 = blue   7 = yellow   8 = green   9 = red   10 = orange

194   Brainy Book of Addition and Subtraction

Page 194

Seeing Spots

Each domino represents a fact family. Write the related facts for each fact family.

$5 + 4 = 9$

$4 + 5 = 9$

$9 - 4 = 5$

$9 - 5 = 4$

$6 + 2 = 8$

$2 + 6 = 8$

$8 - 2 = 6$

$8 - 6 = 2$

Brainy Book of Addition and Subtraction   195

Page 195

Dots and Spots

Each domino represents a fact family. Write the related facts for each fact family.

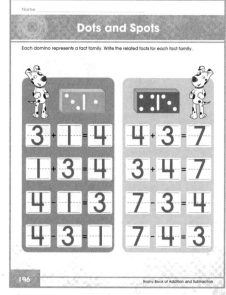

$3 + 1 = 4$

$1 + 3 = 4$

$4 - 1 = 3$

$4 - 3 = 1$

$4 + 3 = 7$

$3 + 4 = 7$

$7 - 3 = 4$

$7 - 4 = 3$

196   Brainy Book of Addition and Subtraction

Page 196

Answer Key

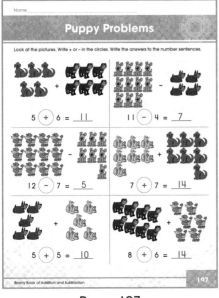

Page 197

Page 198

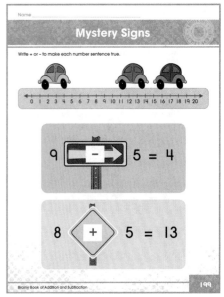

Page 199

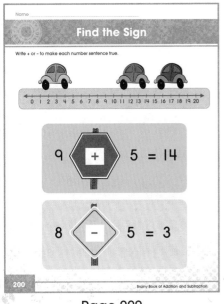

Page 200

Page 201

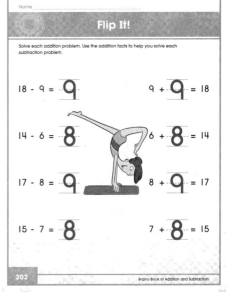

Page 202

Answer Key

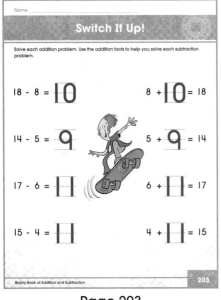

Page 203

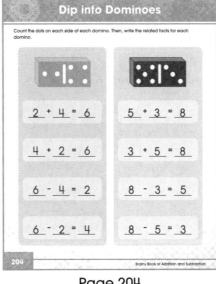

Page 204

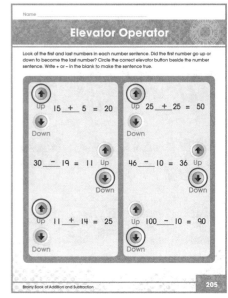

Page 205

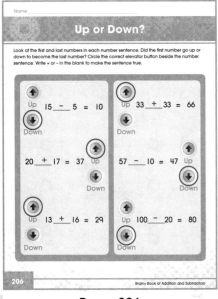

Page 206

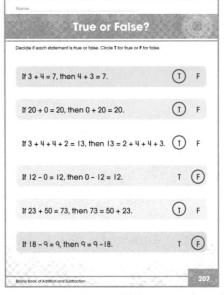

Page 207

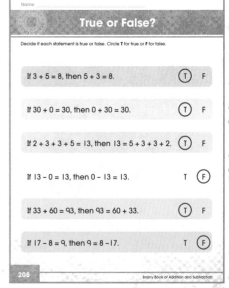

Page 208

Answer Key

Page 209

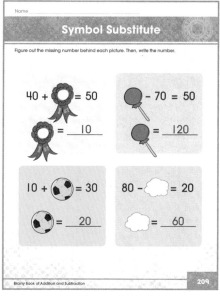

Symbol Substitute

Figure out the missing number behind each picture. Then, write the number.

40 + 🎀 = 50

🎀 = **10**

🏓 − 70 = 50

🏓 = **120**

10 + ⚽ = 30

⚽ = **20**

80 − ☁ = 20

☁ = **60**

Brainy Book of Addition and Subtraction   209

Page 210

Find the Number

Figure out the missing number behind each picture. Then, write the number.

30 + 🎀 = 70

🎀 = **40**

🏓 − 60 = 30

🏓 = **90**

20 + ⚽ = 40

⚽ = **20**

90 − ☁ = 60

☁ = **30**

210   *Brainy Book of Addition and Subtraction*

Page 211

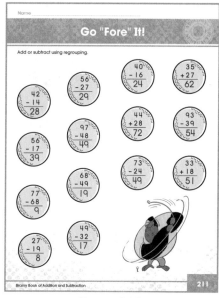

Go "Fore" It!

Add or subtract using regrouping.

$$\begin{array}{r} 42 \\ -14 \\ \hline 28 \end{array} \quad \begin{array}{r} 56 \\ -27 \\ \hline 29 \end{array} \quad \begin{array}{r} 40 \\ -16 \\ \hline 24 \end{array} \quad \begin{array}{r} 35 \\ +27 \\ \hline 62 \end{array}$$

$$\begin{array}{r} 56 \\ -17 \\ \hline 39 \end{array} \quad \begin{array}{r} 97 \\ -48 \\ \hline 49 \end{array} \quad \begin{array}{r} 44 \\ +28 \\ \hline 72 \end{array} \quad \begin{array}{r} 93 \\ -39 \\ \hline 54 \end{array}$$

$$\begin{array}{r} 77 \\ -68 \\ \hline 9 \end{array} \quad \begin{array}{r} 68 \\ -49 \\ \hline 19 \end{array} \quad \begin{array}{r} 73 \\ -24 \\ \hline 49 \end{array} \quad \begin{array}{r} 33 \\ +18 \\ \hline 51 \end{array}$$

$$\begin{array}{r} 27 \\ -19 \\ \hline 8 \end{array} \quad \begin{array}{r} 49 \\ -32 \\ \hline 17 \end{array}$$

Brainy Book of Addition and Subtraction   211

Page 212

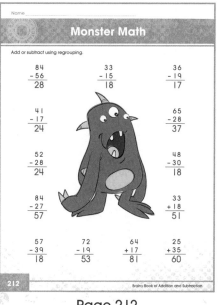

Monster Math

Add or subtract using regrouping.

$$\begin{array}{r} 84 \\ -56 \\ \hline 28 \end{array} \quad \begin{array}{r} 33 \\ -15 \\ \hline 18 \end{array} \quad \begin{array}{r} 36 \\ -19 \\ \hline 17 \end{array}$$

$$\begin{array}{r} 41 \\ -17 \\ \hline 24 \end{array} \quad \begin{array}{r} 65 \\ -28 \\ \hline 37 \end{array}$$

$$\begin{array}{r} 52 \\ -28 \\ \hline 24 \end{array} \quad \begin{array}{r} 48 \\ -30 \\ \hline 18 \end{array}$$

$$\begin{array}{r} 84 \\ -27 \\ \hline 57 \end{array} \quad \begin{array}{r} 33 \\ +18 \\ \hline 51 \end{array}$$

$$\begin{array}{r} 57 \\ -39 \\ \hline 18 \end{array} \quad \begin{array}{r} 72 \\ -19 \\ \hline 53 \end{array} \quad \begin{array}{r} 64 \\ +17 \\ \hline 81 \end{array} \quad \begin{array}{r} 25 \\ +35 \\ \hline 60 \end{array}$$

212   *Brainy Book of Addition and Subtraction*

Page 213

Adding Hundreds

Solve the problems.

3 hundreds	300	6 hundreds	600	
+ 1 hundreds	+ 100	+ 2 hundreds	+ 200	
4 hundreds	**400**	hundreds	800	

$$\begin{array}{r} 200 \\ +200 \\ \hline 400 \end{array} \quad \begin{array}{r} 100 \\ +700 \\ \hline 800 \end{array} \quad \begin{array}{r} 600 \\ +300 \\ \hline 900 \end{array} \quad \begin{array}{r} 400 \\ +500 \\ \hline 900 \end{array}$$

$$\begin{array}{r} 300 \\ +400 \\ \hline 700 \end{array} \quad \begin{array}{r} 800 \\ +100 \\ \hline 900 \end{array} \quad \begin{array}{r} 400 \\ +400 \\ \hline 800 \end{array} \quad \begin{array}{r} 700 \\ +200 \\ \hline 900 \end{array}$$

$$\begin{array}{r} 500 \\ +100 \\ \hline 600 \end{array} \quad \begin{array}{r} 100 \\ +600 \\ \hline 700 \end{array} \quad \begin{array}{r} 500 \\ +200 \\ \hline 700 \end{array} \quad \begin{array}{r} 300 \\ +200 \\ \hline 500 \end{array}$$

$$\begin{array}{r} 300 \\ +300 \\ \hline 600 \end{array} \quad \begin{array}{r} 400 \\ +200 \\ \hline 600 \end{array} \quad \begin{array}{r} 300 \\ +500 \\ \hline 800 \end{array} \quad \begin{array}{r} 200 \\ +100 \\ \hline 300 \end{array}$$

Brainy Book of Addition and Subtraction   213

Page 214

Building Numbers

Look at the examples. Follow the steps to add.

Example:

hundreds	tens	ones		hundreds	tens	ones		hundreds	tens	ones
	1				1				1	
3	4	8		3	4	8		3	4	8
+ 4	4	4		+ 4	4	4		+ 4	4	4
		2			9	2		7	9	2

$$\begin{array}{r} 271 \\ +419 \\ \hline 690 \end{array} \quad \begin{array}{r} 345 \\ +439 \\ \hline 784 \end{array} \quad \begin{array}{r} 609 \\ +244 \\ \hline 853 \end{array} \quad \begin{array}{r} 537 \\ +109 \\ \hline 646 \end{array}$$

$$\begin{array}{r} 418 \\ +323 \\ \hline 741 \end{array} \quad \begin{array}{r} 471 \\ +319 \\ \hline 790 \end{array} \quad \begin{array}{r} 334 \\ +528 \\ \hline 862 \end{array}$$

$$\begin{array}{r} 659 \\ +127 \\ \hline 786 \end{array} \quad \begin{array}{r} 736 \\ +145 \\ \hline 881 \end{array} \quad \begin{array}{r} 426 \\ +165 \\ \hline 591 \end{array}$$

214   *Brainy Book of Addition and Subtraction*

Page 215

Chalk It Up!

Solve the problems. Regroup when needed.

348 + 214 562	172 + 418 590	
623 + 268 891	369 + 533 902	
733 + 229 962	411 + 299 710	423 + 169 592
624 + 368 992	272 + 469 741	393 + 418 811

215

Brainy Book of Addition and Subtraction

Page 216

Problem Solving

Solve each problem.

Example:

Ria packed 300 boxes.
Melvin packed 200 boxes.
How many boxes did Ria and Melvin pack?

200
+300
500

Santo typed 500 letters.
Hale typed 400 letters.
How many letters did they type?

500
+400
900

Paula used 100 paper clips.
Milton used 600 paper clips.
How many paper clips did they use?

100
+600
700

The grocery store sold 400 red apples.
The grocery store also sold 100 yellow apples.
How many apples did the grocery store sell in all?

400
+100
500

216 Brainy Book of Addition and Subtraction

Page 217

Subtracting Hundreds

Solve the problems.

9 hundreds – 7 hundreds 2 hundreds	900 – 700 **200**	3 hundreds – 1 hundreds 2 hundreds	300 – 100 200
700 – 300 400	500 – 400 100	900 – 400 500	800 – 500 300
600 – 100 500	900 – 200 700	500 – 100 400	400 – 200 200
600 – 500 100	300 – 200 100	500 – 100 400	800 – 200 600

Brainy Book of Addition and Subtraction 217

Page 218

Scoops of Fun

Look at the example. Follow the steps to subtract.

Example:
Step 1: Regroup the ones if needed.
Step 2: Subtract the ones.
Step 3: Subtract the tens.
Step 4: Subtract the hundreds.

hundreds	tens	ones
4	5	12
2	5	3
2	0	9

423 – 114 309	562 – 349 213	478 – 239 239	651 – 333 318

Draw a line to the correct answer. Color the ice-cream cones.

347 – 218 = 129
144 – 135 = 9
963 – 748 = 215
762 – 553 = 209
287 – 179 = 108

218 Brainy Book of Addition and Subtraction

Page 219

Bowl 'Em Over

Subtract. Circle the 7s that appear in the 10s place.

Example:
492
– 221
2⑦1

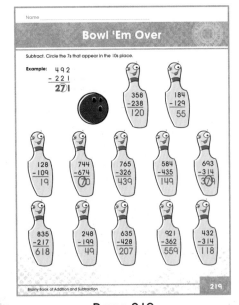

358 – 238 = 120
184 – 129 = 55
128 – 109 = 19
744 – 674 = ⑦0
765 – 326 = 439
584 – 435 = 149
693 – 314 = 3⑦9
835 – 217 = 618
248 – 199 = 49
635 – 428 = 207
921 – 362 = 559
432 – 314 = 118

Brainy Book of Addition and Subtraction 219

Page 220

Add and Subtract

Solve each problem.

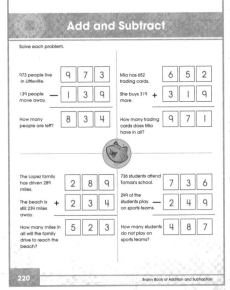

973 people live in Littleville. **973**
139 people move away. **– 139**
How many people are left? **834**

Mia has 652 trading cards. **652**
She buys 319 more. **+ 319**
How many trading cards does Mia have in all? **971**

The Lopez family has driven 289 miles. **289**
The beach is still 234 miles away. **+ 234**
How many miles in all will the family drive to reach the beach? **523**

736 students attend Tomas's school. **736**
249 of the students play on sports teams. **– 249**
How many students do not play on sports teams? **487**

220 Brainy Book of Addition and Subtraction